The Dancer's Complete Guide to Healthcare and a Long Career

Allan J. Ryan, M.D.
Robert E. Stephens, Ph.D.

A Dance Horizons Book

Princeton Book Company, Publishers
Princeton, NJ

A Dance Horizons Book
Princeton Book Company, Publishers
POB 57
Pennington, NJ 08534

Library of Congress Catalog Card Number: 88-71330

International Standard Book Number: 0-916622-79-7

Cover Photo: Left—Robert Stephens in "Baroque Variations"
              Right—Jessica Stulik

Printed in the United States of America

To Toni Lander Marks—
whose artistry, inspiration, and dignity is
our legacy of what a dancer can be and humans should be.
And to the dancers with the brightest hope
for healthy and long careers.

CONTENTS

FOREWORD

Dance is the human body. Dance is now. No one knows that more than the people who do it, the dancers. It is for precious little worldly gain these "Acrobats of God" set out as small children to shape and reshape their instruments so that they might play the most sublime choreographic music. Imagine if you will the violinist working daily to build and rebuild his Stradivarius. Unthinkable? The dancer does so daily with the knowledge that at any moment some part may break down, with the understanding that if all things do go well there may be only a few years of peak performance. If goals that are difficult to attain are to be prized then the unrealistic aspiration of a life in dance must be one of the most worthy of all.

It is not surprising then that dancers cannot and will not think of the long term. Given what they know and see around them there is very little that is permanent. Weight is always a concern and eating disorders can become the rule rather than the exception. Dancers are often hired and fired within a short time. Injuries end a career in an instant. Directors who are perhaps as fearful of the future as are the dancers make impossible demands for short term results. Everywhere we are told that "the show must go on".

There is no doubt that the show will go on. The question is how much are you, the dancers, willing to jeopardize the long term... your career, to have the show go on. We all know that the competition these days is fierce and that stress on a young artist is almost unbearable. It is time to remove that stress with the understanding that reason must prevail. Maturity is perhaps a great deal to ask of a young artist who indeed may have been attracted to a life in dance because it is so marvelously impractical. If, however, getting the most out of the wonderful life that is a career in dance is your aim then there is no other way than to take care of the instrument and the being that controls that instrument.

Some years ago when I was running a summer school in Aspen a young ballet student approached the Danish Ballerina Toni Lander and, looking up at her, asked. "Miss Lander, am I going to make it?" Toni looked shocked and told the young dancer that the question was really not appropriate. Toni asked the youngster if she loved what she was doing and the little girl replied, "Oh, more than anything in the world". Toni smiled as she said, "most people go through life never having found something to do that they truly love. Don't you see that you've already made it?"

For those of you who have found a passion for this most demanding of art forms, this book is invaluable. It will enable you to live up to the demands that will be placed on you and even more the demands that you must place on yourself. Even more importantly it will help you to achieve your maximum potential with confidence and joy.

Bruce Marks
Artistic Director
Boston Ballet
August 1988

PROLOGUE

Dance is a merciless master and dancers are its captive slaves. Mesmerized by the art and form of human movement, they dance, ever younger and stronger, with greater daring and skill. They dance for themselves and then for others. Entranced in the challenge, puzzled by the nuance, elated by the delicately balanced beauty of dance movement, they dance with joy, pleasure and youthful indifference to the specter of pain.

They see other dancers whose careers were tragically shortened by injury and they see not the slightest image of themselves. Youth remains in mind what the body has long since forgotten. Yet, it is difficult for any young dancer to face the potential hazards of dancing and do anything about them. Young dancers are generally not interested or threatened by the prospect of injury. To admit this hazard is to face one's own vulnerability—something that even adults are reluctant to do.

Yet, we must face this need to care for dancers—an irreplaceable artistic resource. We as a society owe it to ourselves to assure the creation, development and promotion of dance. It is a collective responsibility. Schools and companies often shirk this obligation as being too expensive or impractical; it is neither. Tossing the responsibility onto young dancers is abandonment and negligent. Health care and injury prevention techniques should be an integral part of *all* dance training.

It is unfortunate that injuries are part and parcel of the "weeding out" process in many schools and companies. Some teachers actually rationalize this tragic waste of talent, training and art as a Darwinian survival of the fittest. They figure that the demands and rigors of the technique will sort out the best dancers for the art. One would have thought that this type of archaic reasoning had died with the forced marches of many a failed military campaign; perhaps the "best" soldiers survived, but they were often the worse for wear. Professional dancers too can be a battle weary lot when they have to carry the banner, "All for technique, technique not for all."

When the dance community fails to protect and care for the health and well-being of the dancer, dancers are often left on their own to deal with the confusing and disconcerting world of medicine. Although physicians and health professionals have made an effort to address the special needs of dancers, much more must be done.

The Dancer's Complete Guide to Healthcare and a Long Career is intended to meet many of the basic needs and concerns of the dancer, and serve as a guide into and out of the maze of common health and medical problems. We are confident that the information in this book, when properly and consistently practiced, will enhance the quality and increase the longevity of a dancer's career.

The first part is devoted to a discussion of the dancer's environment, physical characteristics, training and nutrition. Any serious dancer will appreciate the importance of this fundamental material. Dr. Ryan has also compiled a thorough survey of general medical problems, health and nutritional concerns, and dance-related injuries. A few dancers will find some of this material too technical; others will seek much more. We feel we have reached a reasonable compromise by adding a Glossary of Medical Terms and Glossary of Dance Terms at the end of the book and by referring the more advanced reader to our parent text, *Dance Medicine: A Comprehensive Guide* (Pluribus Press and The Physician and Sportsmedicine, 1987).

The latter half of this book is dedicated to teaching the dancer about the causes, treatment, rehabilitation and prevention of a wide variety of dance-related injuries. *The Dancer's Guide* was intended to be just that—a guide, and not a substitute for medical care and treatment. Although we believe that we have covered the majority of injuries and health concerns relevant to dancers, dancers and companies continue to conjure up new and more bizarre ways to abuse the human body and stress the spirit.

It is one thing to say that there are too many injuries in dance or that dancers are too skinny, it is quite another to do something about it. *The Dancer's Guide* concentrates heavily upon useful concepts, techniques and methods of preventing injuries in dance. Most of these injuries can be prevented if they are interpreted within the framework of the cycle of injury (chapter 12). The majority of career-disabling injuries have been repetitive or chronic problems for months or years before halting a dancer's career in mid-track. Failing to determine the cause of an injury or diminishing the quality of treatment or rehabilitation steers the dancer directly into the path of an oncoming injury. In a sense we are teaching dancers to be better drivers by breaking down the cause-effect relationship of dance injuries and showing dancers how to determine the cause of their injury and apply specific injury prevention techniques to the situation.

We have devoted much of our professional careers to helping dancers and their art. Our experiences as a dancer/scientist and a physician/surgeon are brought to bear in *The Dancer's Guide,* and are shared with the highest esteem and respect for our friends, colleagues and patients who embody the essence of dance. It has always been true that the legacy of dance is lasting images of dancers; forms and figures casting graceful lines of poetic images and movement. This book is for today's dancers with the brightest hope for healthy and long careers.

Robert E. Stephens, Ph.D.
Kansas City, MO

Allan J. Ryan, M.D.
Minneapolis, MN

1

THE DANCER'S WORLD

Participation in dance can be the harshest look in the mirror an individual will ever make. Youth, health, beauty and physical performance seem to ferment the type of creative energy, narcissism and personal discipline necessary to excel in the highly competitive dance world. To survive and ascend, a dancer must be self-analytical and self-critical virtually to a fault. For dancers, dance is more than an art; it is an all-consuming lifestyle. The aesthetic, the technique, the teachers, and perhaps most importantly, the dancer must constantly push to exceed, to overcome, to persist and to persevere.

The love of dance and desire to dance are intrinsic to dancers of all levels and talent. Many have sacrificed so much just to have those few moments of pure movement where the physical price was no measure of the artistic reward. Dance is, indeed, a competitive world, and every individual should thoroughly understand exactly what they are getting into when he or she decides to try to become a dancer.

Although dance technique is a highly evolved art and science, not all dance techniques and styles have ascended the same evolutionary tree. In any discussion of dance, the word *ballet* has become synonymous with dance. Often, this usage has been to the exclusion of other equally valid forms of dance such as modern, jazz or ethnic. Ballet is not the generic word for dance. Ballet is more familiar to the general public because of its longer history and higher profile in the various media.

Over the last 400 years, several major schools of technique have disseminated from the stylized court dances of Catherine de Medici and Louis XIV. The powerful Russian style radiating from the famous Vaganova school in Leningrad, the highly-structured Cecchetti method based in London at the Royal Ballet School, the buoyant Bournonville style at the Royal Danish Ballet, the fleet-footed Balanchine style from the American School of Ballet, and the elegant French school from the *Ecole de Danse du Theatre National de l'Opera* form the historical, artistic and pedagogical heritage of modern ballet. These courtly origins have also been the genesis for new types of dance, or the reason to find new forms, patterns and styles of movement—some of which may be more expressive or more natural to the body. Whatever type or style of dance you choose, the process of ascending the ladder to the rank of professional dancer is basically the same.

The Hierarchy of Dance

The hierarchy of dance starts with the thousands of local dance studios at the base of the pyramid followed by university dance departments, the pre-professional dance schools which are usually affiliated with a dance company, and lastly, at the very apex, the dance companies. Dance companies may be non-professional, semi-professional or professional depending upon payment for the dancer's services and, to a lesser degree, the dancer's membership in a labor union. The dancers in smaller civic dance companies are usually unpaid or paid per performance; whereas the dancers in regional and national companies are usually paid for rehearsals and performances or receive a salary. In most ballet companies dancers are ranked as principals, soloists, corps de ballet, or apprentices according to their artistry, expertise and seniority. Since the workloads and responsibilities may vary from one rank to another, there may be differences in the incidence of injury.

Out of hundreds of thousands of young dancers, only a very select few will become professional dancers. There are probably only about 500 positions for dancers in the major ballet companies in the United States, and, perhaps, a few hundred additional jobs in regional and civic companies. Not all of these jobs pay enough for the dancer to live on all year around. The competition for those few elite positions in the best companies such as the New York City Ballet, American Ballet Theatre, and San Francisco Ballet is extremely severe. It is not unusual for a dancer to continue to dance in spite of his injuries, because of the extreme competition for employment and dancing roles in the few major ballet companies.

In the major ballet companies the dancer's obligations to the company, and in some instances the company's responsibility to the dancer, are under the careful surveillance of dance unions such as the American Guild of Musical Artists (AGMA). In many respects companies such as the New York City Ballet, American Ballet Theatre, San Francisco Ballet, Ballet West, Boston Ballet and Houston Ballet not only represent the pinnacle of ballet, but they are the financial centers of dance in America. The conditions under which injuries occur in the various studios, schools and companies within the hierarchy of dance varies considerably, depending upon the company philosophy, leadership, and financial stability. A few companies try to create a healthy and productive environment for their dancers. Most companies, however, still consider and treat dancers as if they were commodities in a supply-side market.

Ballet companies may induce dancers to perform under hazardous conditions or with injuries through implied and real threats to their jobs. In these circumstances dancer's unions such as the American Guild of Musical Artists (AGMA) may offer some support. However, there are other ways to motivate dancers. In the major ballet companies the dancers are quite aware that there is a reservoir of younger—generally healthier—dancers in the company-affiliated school. Senior student dancers usually learn much of the basic corps and soloist repertoire either on their own or in class (i.e., at no expense to the company), and may even serve as apprentices to the company. The company's hole card is this pre-rehearsed, dance-like-there-is-no-tomorrow senior class. There is always another dancer in the wings ready and eager to step in at a moment's notice.

There are more clever ways of motivating an injured dancer to perform. For example, while the company is on tour other dancers may consciously or unconsciously encourage the disabled dancer to perform. They are well aware that his absence would increase their workload and their chance of injury. If the other dancers are successful at convincing the injured dancer to perform, they remain healthy while the injured dancer develops chronic disability and must stop dancing. Eventually, the other dancers will get the disabled dancer's roles when they return home from the tour.

Training and Workload

A dancer's training has few rivals in the art or sport world in terms of duration, frequency and intensity. Training to become a ballet dancer is like a young boy taking batting and fielding practice six days a week, all year around from the age of eight to 17. Serious ballet training typically begins at the age of eight for females, but somewhat later for males (exhibit 1-1). The tendency for American boys to start ballet training four to nine years later than girls probably reflects the sociocultural bias against dance as an acceptable occupation for men. However, the emergence of powerful positive role models in dance such as Mikhail Baryshnikov and Peter Martins has answered many of the public's doubts about the validity and masculinity of studying dance.

Over the course of about ten years of training the young dancer takes more and more 90-minute classes per week at progressively greater levels of intensity and proficiency. During this time, dancers may train in one particular style of ballet such as Cecchetti, Russian or Bournonville, although most ballet dancers study more than one style. In addition, most dancers also train in modern, jazz and character dance. Similarly, dancers in each of these other dance disciplines also commonly cross-train in other techniques and styles.

Dance is a hierarchical profession, and it makes a huge difference whether one is studying at a local civic ballet company or at the American Ballet Theatre. The type or style of dance as well as the caliber of dancer are important factors in the development and prevalence of certain types of dance injuries. Whether it is Balanchine or Cecchetti techniques in ballet, Graham or Horton in modern, Tremaine or Fosse in jazz, Georgian or Spanish in character dancing, each style places a particular demand on the human body, and may therefore contribute in some manner to the overall incidence of injury in a specific group of dancers. Generally, it has not been proven that one particular type of style of dance is more injurious than another. There are, however, slight differences in the distribution of injuries to various regions of the body. In the most cases the greatest hazards are associated with the way in which the work environment is controlled by the teacher, director, or choreographer.

Selection for the ballet schools affiliated with the top companies occurs rather early in this training process, and forces the adolescent to make a commitment to the dance. While their peers are

Exhibit 1-1
Training Histories of Ballet Dancers*

| | Professional Dancers | | Student Dancers | |
	Men	Women	Men	Women
Number of dancers	15	24	11	71
Starting age in dance	12.3±4.2	8.6±2.1	16.3±2.1	7.3±3.4
Total years of dancing	13.0±4.8	12.7±3.6	4.0±2.7	8.2±2.8
Years at this level	7.2±3.4	5.1±2.2	0.7±1.1	2.7±1.2

Exhibit 1-2
Work Load of Ballet Dancers*

Dancers	Class	Rehearsal	Performance	Total
Female professionals N = 24	10.2±2.3	26.6±6.1	7.9±3.6	44.7±4.0
Male professionals N = 15	9.3±0.9	26.1±6.2	9.5±5.3	44.9±4.1
Female students N = 71	13.6±6.1	**	**	**
Male students N = 11	17.3±7.7	**	**	**

*In average hours of participation per week
**Rehearsal and performance work loads for advanced students were
  not included.

worrying about pimples and dates, young talented dancers are faced with a crucial career choice. Since many companies take the majority of their new dancers from their affiliated dance schools, it can be difficult, although not impossible, for a novice to enter the ranks of a large ballet company unless he or she has progressed through the school. More latitude exists in this regard in smaller companies and in other forms of dance, such as modern and jazz. Although a dancer may believe it was tough getting into a company, it may be far more difficult to survive its grueling schedules and constant pressures.

Dancers should always be aware of the of physical risks involved in dancing during the course of a week, month, season or year. This means keeping a complete training record of the number of hours a day devoted to class, rehearsal and performance, the number of performances a week or in a season, and the number and length of each season in a year. This record can be invaluable in the determination of overuse injuries and the assessment of causes of injuries. In addition, certain dance styles may influence the occurrence of injuries, and it is helpful to know which ones influence the training and choreography.

A typical work schedule during a season for a professional ballet dancer includes 9 hours in class, about 26 hours in rehearsal, and 8–12 hours in performance for a total of 43–48 hours during a six-day period (exhibit 1-2). The standard union contract is 36 weeks per year, but varies according to the tour schedules and bookings. The contract year is subdivided into three or four seasons, each one having a varying number of rehearsals and performances. In many professional companies the rehearsal and performance workload as well as working conditions are specified in the dancer's contract and monitored by the union.

In dance studios and schools there is, of course, no union to protect the student from his or her own youthful ambition to dance more and more. Studies of advanced female students indicate that they spend approximately 14 hours a week in class, which was generally reported as two classes per day on a five-day schedule. Some male students spent as many as 30 hours per week in class. This disproportionate classroom workload of some of the male students reflects their desire to accomplish specific goals in a shorter period of time, and probably contributes to their rapid accumulation of injuries so early in their careers.

Your training workload should be closely monitored by your teacher and you. Depending upon your age, ability, and previous training, 12–16 hours of classroom training in a particular type of dance is probably optimal. A few hours of other types of dance training may be added if you are in good condition and not too fatigued.

On Being a Dancer

What is it like to be a professional dancer? Is it glamorous, exciting, or just ego-gratifying? The virtues of being a dancer are all of these things and more. There is enormous satisfaction and personal reward in the gradual evolution into the world of dancing. Only a dancer can fully appreciate the intricacies of the struggles with technique, the meaning of a particular movement in relation to music, and the thrill of artistic creativity and expression. Being a dancer is everything, but easy, painless, and lucrative. Without any doubt, dancing is hard work with many physical and financial risks.

> A 28 year-old male soloist dancer in a major professional ballet company came to me for consultation. His chief complaint was severe pain in the lateral aspect of his left leg during jumps. Point tenderness was present on the fibula approximately 6 inches above the ankle. Biomechanical evaluations indicated that he had tight hip muscles, that limited his turnout. This was more prominent on the left. He admitted to forcing his turnout at the feet in order to compensate. The training history indicated that the pain began six months previously while performing on a hard stage in Denver, Colorado, and that he had been dancing steadily ever since. It was concluded that the pain was caused by excessively tight hip muscles, forcing the turnout, dancing on the hard stage floor, and the heavy workload. He was referred to a physician, and a diagnosis of a fibular stress fracture was made after bone scans.
> Four months later I was contacted by the dancer who was suing the state's Workmen's Compensation Board for lost wages during his recovery. Since the injury did not occur at a *finite* place and time relative to work, the board claimed the ballet company owed no compensation. I prepared a statement documenting the workload and physical demands of his occupation. It read in conclusion:

Without any doubt, Mr. W sustained his injury while dancing, not jogging or playing tennis. The issue of the time of onset is irrelevant, since there are many infamous precedents for awarding compensation for long-term exposure to occupational hazards. When did the coal miner get black lung disease? On the first or ten thousandth inhalation? Or the asbestos worker asbestosis? The board seems to be saying to dancers, 'When you get a real job in the real world and become a real person, we'll talk about real compensation.' What we are witnessing is selective discrimination against dance as a serious occupation for adults.

Because of his unwillingness to accept the inequities of the system, this bold dancer settled his dispute and established a precedent for fair and equitable job treatment for all dancers in the state. After his recovery, he worked hard to incorporate effective injury prevention techniques and exercises into his training, and he was promoted to principal dancer. As of today, he is still performing.

As a slice of a performer's life, this story is both typical and atypical at the same time. It is typical in the fact that professional dance is not without some physical risks. Indeed, some of these injuries may be temporarily or permanently disabling, and result in serious financial problems for the dancer. Staying healthy and making a living are primary concerns of a dancer.

What is unusual about this story is that the dancer decided to do something about his situation. The dance world is not immutable and permanent. It can change (as it has in the past and will in the future) when dancers, either individually or collectively, make a stand on issues which are important to their livelihood and artistry. All too often, dancers are passive participants in the decisions that rule their lives and art. Whether it is the issue of fair and equitable employment practices, or the providing of adequate medical benefits, dancers should have a significant say so in the decision-making process. Unfortunately, these issues are often left to the "bottom line" mentality of the board of directors or administrators. Dancing may be voiceless, dancers are not.

2

THE DANCER'S BODY

Over the centuries dance has evolved into a highly structured and stylized art. Each of the forms of dance—ballet, modern and jazz—have developed specific techniques and styles. They also have somewhat differing concepts of the most appropriate image of the dancer. Appropriate in this sense refers to the shape, function, aesthetic merits and marketability of the dancer's body. Dance does not require a particular physique—audiences do.

From one era to another societies establish their own concept of the most acceptable body types. Just how and why a society creates and encourages these standards is a mystery. Nevertheless, they (whoever "they" may be) do. The result is not always flattering, enlightening, reassuring or progressive to its bearers. In the twentieth century dancers, fashion models and athletes have continuously been the prototypes and stereotypes of society's analytical, capricious gaze.

The major point that is lost in all arguments on the image of the dancer is that image may be important to the dancer, but it is not a critical factor to dance. Beyond certain obvious physical limitations of structure and function, such as morbid obesity or paralysis, individuals should be allowed to dance if they are so inclined. No one may buy a ticket to see them, but that does not disqualify it as dance or them as dancers.

A desirable dancer's physique can be a curious invention of form and function as well as art and society. Although dancers come in a variety of sizes, there are certain arbitrary norms for the performing dancer. According to Peter Martins, choreographer and co-ballet master in chief of the New York City Ballet,

> As far as dancers are concerned, I'm still going to hire
> dancers that look best in Balanchine ballets. I happen to

> like that look in a dancer myself. Where I may differ is
> in that I like a more individualistic dancer. And yet Ba-
> lanchine also liked different kinds of physiques and per-
> sonalities.... We have always liked different kinds of
> dancers, different ways of moving, different approaches
> to things. Obviously, when you have a corps de ballet,
> you have to have a certain uniformity, but we are big
> enough to absorb a few people who are different from
> the rest.... The world thinks that the New York City
> Ballet has a particular policy...on shape or sort or size.
> [Such a policy] simply doesn't exist.

These are inspiring words from the director of one of the best companies in the world. Yet, I would hardly classify the appearance of the City Ballet dancers as a diverse population. They may be distinct and different in character and personality, but not in shape and style. The only thing that is obvious about the "ideal" body type is its capricious dependence upon the "artistic vision" of the teacher or director.

The image of the female ballerina has changed considerably from the early nineteenth to the late twentieth century. The full-figured ballerina of the Romantic era has been dropped in favor of the ultralean, long-limbed dancer that was demanded by the late director of the New York City Ballet, George Balanchine. In all fairness to Mr. Balanchine, his images of dancers were merely riding the crest of a trend in society, fashion, sports and dance towards skinny, prepubescent role models.

Physical Characteristics

Many different dance styles, from ballet to folk dance, are practiced by an even wider variety of body types. Dance is for anyone who has the feeling and desire and capacity for movement. Beautiful movement is not necessarily a function of a particular body type. On the other hand, whether or not people will pay to see chubby ballerinas punish their toes is a practical sociocultural issue of some concern to the aspiring performer. Over the centuries, dancers have always changed their forms in order to conform to the aesthetic ideals of a particular individual or society. The transformation of the dancer into present-day ultralean androgynous form can be traced to the Romantic ballets of the early nineteenth century. Although these early ballerinas would be unliftable by today's standards, they nevertheless sought the illusion of a fragile, ethereal sylph. This trend persists in the dreams of most dancers and the gaunt reality of a few.

Young dancers should understand that the image of the tall, lean, narrow-hipped, long-limbed ballet dancer is not universally accepted in the dance world. There are thousands of wonderful dancers in many disciplines who hardly fit into this restrictive mold. Some dancers ignore and scorn such arbitrary barriers to the learning, creation, performance and enjoyment of dance movement. However, physicians should be acutely aware of the dancer's preoccupation with thinness and body image when evaluating or discussing the amount of body fat in a dancer. Leanness is not only an artistic standard in many professional dance companies: it is an occupational absolute! Dancers constantly strive to perfect the form of the human body while struggling with the trials of dance technique.

A number of scientific studies have been done on professional dancers from international, national and regional ballet companies. What is clear in all of these reports is the amazing degree of homogeneity in the overall physical characteristics of elite ballet dancers. The average female dancer in these companies was 23 years old, 5 foot 5-1/2 inches, 107 pounds, with 13–16 percent body fat. The male dancers were 27 years old, 5 foot 10 inches, 153 pounds, with 8–13 percent body fat (see exhibit 2-1). Obviously, the leanness of professional ballet dancers is comparable to that of elite non-endurance athletes. Advanced students in the major ballet schools and studios also tend to approach these figures.

Almost any dance company has examples of dancers who excel in spite of the fact that they do not fit within the physical norm. Perhaps they are a bit bosomy, a little shorter or thicker in the thighs, but they succeed despite some pretty fierce odds. By today's standards, these individuals represent the exception rather than the rule, and they know their career limitations and vulnerabilities very well. The major task of the "nonstandard" ballet dancer is slipping through the cattle-sorting at the beginning of a school or company audition and getting a chance to dance. The chances of this happening are roughly inversely proportional to the status of the school, studio or company.

Certain styles of dance may favor particular body types. Small, light bodies are favored in dances that require great agility, flexibil-

Exhibit 2-1
Physical Characteristics of Ballet Dancers

Dancers	Age	Height*	Weight**	Percent Body Fat
Female professionals N = 24	22.6 ± 3.7	166.1 ± 4.3	48.7 ± 3.6	15.7 ± 1.2
Male professionals N = 15	27.3 ± 5.6	178.1 ± 3.3	69.4 ± 5.5	13.0 ± 2.3
Female students N = 77	16.0 ± 1.8	163.6 ± 4.3	47.4 ± 5.6	16.6 ± 1.5
Male students N = 11	21.0 ± 2.9	178.3 ± 6.9	65.5 ± 8.5	11.7 ± 2.9

*In centimeters
**In kilograms

ity and jumping. Those that employ acrobatic techniques also require quickness of movement and good balance, qualities more easily developed and maintained by slender individuals. An athletic physique is advantageous in big jumps and lifting. Obesity to any degree is a handicap to a dancer, even it if does not present an aesthetic problem. Extra weight from general muscle development should not be a problem because of the strength and power it makes possible.

An accurate assessment of body composition to determine the relative amount of body fat and lean tissue such as muscle and bone is important to dancers and their supervisors. Knowing your body composition can often eliminate meaningless comparisons of body fat percentages and the omnipresent dancer's indictment, "You're too fat." If you have your body fat analyzed by one of these methods, you should keep in mind that the optimal and typical percentage body fat for female and male professional dancers is about 16 percent and 12 percent, respectively.

A variety of instruments and techniques for assessing body composition (including the amount of body fat and lean body mass) are generally available at most health clubs, physical education departments, and sports medicine facilities. These methods may use skinfold calipers, bioelectrical impedance equipment, ultrasonic devices, or hydrostatic (underwater) weighing tanks. All of these techniques and instruments have their advantages and disadvantages in terms of time, convenience, simplicity and expense. Nevertheless, despite the claims of the manufacturers, all of these devices have about the same degree of accuracy ($\pm$ 4 percent). Skinfold calipers are probably the most widely used instrument for determining body fat, and can be simple, fast and accurate in the hands of an experienced examiner.

As a dancer you should be interested in assessing your proportion of body fat and lean body mass through one of these established methods. It is foolish and quite possibly dangerous to arbitrarily arrive at an "ideal" body weight without this assessment. Height/weight charts, such as in Chapter 8, may be generally helpful, but they do not take into account the variety of body types which are possible at each height. Both height and skeletal frame size are determined by your genes with varying degrees of positive and negative influence for external factors such as nutrition and training. Good balanced nutrition and effective training methods tend to maximize your growth potential. On the other end of the spectrum, poor dietary habits and a "couch potato" existence pretty much limit the possibility for a tutu in your dancing future.

What may be true for ballet may not be true for other forms of dance, but the prospective dancer who plans to establish a career must give some consideration as to where his/her body type may fit best. Once you have achieved full growth in height, which for girls may be as early as 15 years and for boys around 18–21, you're stuck with it. So learn to live with it and find your own niche in dance. Tall and lanky or short and stout, dancers come in a variety of sizes and shapes. For non-professionals, dancing is an expressive way of moving, not a body type; for professional dancers it is a combination of both.

3

MENTAL PERSPECTIVES

Any new activity begins with thinking about the idea or the concept involved and deciding to try it. You may have reasons both for and against which you balance to see whether the results of your decision will bring you pleasure, or perhaps only sorrow and trouble. This process may go on consciously or subconsciously for some time before you decide that it is time to try it.

At that point you look more closely at the prospect of your involvement to find out if you can do it, or at least can make a reasonably good attempt. You may talk with someone who is already involved, read more about it, or take an opportunity to see the activity as a keen observer. Any or all of these things will help to tell you whether you are qualified physically, and just as importantly, whether you are up to it mentally. If you think that you can do it and feel that you want to do it you probably can.

For whatever reason or circumstance you first decided that you wished to become a dancer seriously, your mental outlook must have been shaped by several different but related considerations. Among these there may have been three that were principal: your orientation towards dance as a desirable activity; your thoughts about how it would fit into or cause adjustments in your lifestyle; and your feelings about how you could and would cope with the changes that would be necessary and the problems that you might encounter.

Orientation to Dance

Dance appears innate in children in forms similar to what we see in young animals. It is a means of spontaneous self-expression that even in its most primitive forms tends to assume a repetitive pattern. Depending on the mood or other internal or external circumstances affecting the individual, the pace and intensity may vary from slow and mild to rapid and vigorous. It is inclined to be contagious, provoking a similar activity among others who are present and looking on. The different emerging patterns tend to influence each other, and in the process of many repetitions a more or less uniform pattern may appear. This occurs most commonly in closely related persons, or families, or in communities where children and adults are constantly in close contact.

These primitive unorganized forms of dance activity are gradually shaped by the older individuals in the families or communities into patterns that have special meanings. These meanings may be expressions of love, joy, anger or more subtle emotions; they may express social or religious practices such as celebrations of coming of age or marriage; they may portray cultural or ethnic beliefs or practices; or they may simply convey the wish to amuse or entertain. The younger and more inexperienced learn from the older experienced dancers by imitation or instruction.

The need to express oneself in physical activity becomes channeled into different patterns but still retains its individuality. The improvisation of the individual over time influences the general pattern so that forms develop and change, even in what may appear to be a rather unyielding structure. The particular body image as seen and felt by the individual can express itself in a great variety of forms.

Although dance has been seen by the dancer in the past primarily as a means of self-expression rather than of exercise, recent interest in intensive exercise of moderate duration which is now generally known as aerobic exercise has prompted many people, especially women, to use a series of dance type movements as a means of regular vigorous exercise. All dance is a form of exercise and those who dance regularly can keep themselves physically fit for activities of daily living and other recreational pursuits.

Dance has also been used as a form of therapy for persons who are handicapped physically or by mental or emotional problems. In these cases it appears that the opportunities afforded for self-expression combine with the physical conditioning to produce the therapeutic effect. Motivation to seek this outlet ordinarily comes from without, that is, from another concerned person or agency, and not from within the person who is handicapped.

Some movements and activities of dance closely approximate actions or patterns of movements in sports. In some sports such as gymnastics and figure skating or ice dancing, dance carriage and body movement are an important part of the sport skills and technique. The athlete may think of himself or herself as much as a dancer as an athlete. Some athletes and coaches in other sports have found that instruction and practice of dance skills have helped athletes in their conditioning and performance.

Finally, the strength of a person's orientation towards dance as a desirable activity will be a strong influence on that person's mental outlook towards other demands and activities in life. Conflicts of other interests and demands on personal time may be resolved by the person strongly oriented to dance in favor of that activity to the detriment of other activities which may be of considerable importance. If dance is a career, that is only natural, and should tend to promote reaching career objectives. If it is not a career, it can create problems that can upset the person's mental outlook towards his or her life as a whole.

Adjustment of Lifestyle

In undertaking any new activity you have to consider the time that you have available to pursue it, how it may prevent you from doing things you are used to doing and which you enjoy, how much it will cost, and how it may change the company you keep. Changes involving activities that are only occasional or intermittent and that don't involve serious commitment can usually be accomplished easily. To become seriously involved in dance, however, is to enter a whole new way of life and of living.

You enter gradually or precipitously, depending on the early depth of your involvement, into a new world with a set of values that may be quite different from those to which you are accustomed. You enter a world where people think, talk and act differently, and where although externally imposed discipline may be strict and severe, a powerful self-imposed internal discipline may be even more important. It is a world in which performing art is mixed with business matters, where competition frequently overrides cooperation, and in which what you get out of it depends almost directly on what you put into it.

Whatever level of general or specific education you have reached in life, you must become a perpetual student in a demanding school. It may require you to forego, or at least postpone, other formal education because of its demands on your time and where you must place yourself. It may not lead to your winning diplomas or degrees but it may, if carried far enough, earn you qualification as a professional and recognition by your peers.

One thing that you may find quickly is that if you have enjoyed a circle of friends who are not involved in dance it will be increasingly difficult for you to maintain regular contact with them and continue what may have been a close social relationship. The demands on your time, those that are imposed by others and those that are self-imposed, will make it necessary for you to plan more exactly for time that you can spare for these contacts, and always with the realization that even this time may be taken up at the last moment by some unpredictable event or opportunity that may be important to your dance career. You will also accumulate gradually a circle of acquaintances and friends who are dancers, and may wish to spend much of your free time with them.

Even more important is the possibility that the opportunities for study and practice in dance you are seeking may not be available in the community where you are living. This may require you to move to another city or another state, or in the extreme, to another country. Once there you will become part of a new circle and it will be more difficult to maintain contact with the old ones. Such a move will also be difficult if you have close family attachments, and especially if you are married.

The relationships between the dancer and his or her family are important in the development of the dancer's career, particularly from the standpoint of how the family as a group or as individuals looks upon dance as an avocation or a career. For the very young dancer this is critical because he or she is dependent on the family for physical and financial support. If parents disapprove of dance as a form of study, or ultimately as a career, they are unlikely to arrange or pay for dance lessons, to accommodate the family schedule to the times when these lessons occur or to take the children to and from lessons. They may also be required to pay for special clothing or shoes and purchase tickets for dance performances. The extent of their commitment is similar to what they might have to do for a young athlete, but perhaps greater since dance occurs at all times of the year and does not have a single season as many sports do.

Parents will be seriously concerned about the ways in which any type of activity interferes with their children completing their academic education. Since only a small proportion of those who start dance careers early in life go on to become professionals, the young dance student must continue education to prepare for other possible careers. This means in terms of general education, not necessarily in vocational education. In today's society a high school diploma is a virtual requirement for most jobs. Persons without a college degree will face considerable handicaps in entering a high-level business position or a profession. The better dance schools and academies may require academic studies beyond the field of dance, but the emphasis is more on meeting minimal requirements than a broad general education.

In order to respond to these demands the dancer has to learn very early to organize time efficiently. Scheduling becomes difficult because dance classes and other related instruction have fixed times and other activities have to be arranged around these times. Your hours may be too irregular to allow you to participate in other activities with conflicting times. If you have preferences about doing certain things at particular times of day these feelings may have to be adjusted to utilize the time available to you.

Some dancers are dependent to some degree for their personal finances on part-time employment. It's not impossible to continue this, but if the hours for it are fixed at times in conflict with dance instruction it can be very difficult. If you can set your own hours it is better, depending on where it has to be done. The main problem then may be in allowing adequate time for rest. If you are always tired you can do justice to neither one.

With all this activity you may require a good deal of transportation. This creates an additional demand on your personal finances, whether for public transportation or the maintenance of a car. Children may be able to rely on their parents for much of this, but parents have to consider the cost as well.

Finally, in addition to the changes and adjustments you have to make in your life to undertake a career in dance, you may have to consider the nature of dance as a field for you as an individual who may or may not have a competitive nature. At every level from the beginning the structure of the group in which you are working resembles a pyramid. Recognition and success depend on making your way to the top in spite of the efforts of others in your group who are trying to do the same thing. You have to want very much to do this in the face of this competition. You must not be reluctant to put yourself forward and overcome or ignore the efforts of others to make you feel less worthy.

Coping Behavior

The first feelings that you may have to cope with relate to the attitudes towards dance as an activity and as a career that you see in your own family, among your close friends and other associates, and in the community where you live. Do they see it as an activity that is one of many desirable possibilities, as an avocation or a career? Perhaps some view it as a revolt against conventional ideas of behavior regarding planning or organizing one's future. It might even be seen as a move towards withdrawal from your family or friends because of the demands that it can make on your time and the possible necessity of having to move elsewhere for study or performance.

If you have no doubts about the answers to questions that might be raised by these feelings, you should be able to answer these concerns when they arise. Even better, you may be able to anticipate such concerns by explaining your ideas and plans as they develop. Generally today the performing arts are seen as occupying not only a respectable but even an honorable place in our society.

The demands on your family, if you are still living at home and dependent on them for your support, can be serious concerns to you as well as to them. If they can see that you are serious in your intent and what you will need from them is not beyond their ability to supply, you should be able to work out this relationship. Both you and they will have to give up something to make this possible. Your task will be to see that these things will be replaced by a new relationship that will be equally rewarding.

Your close friends and associates can be reassured by your reminding them that the situation will be little different from that in which you might be going away to a university in some distant city. You would keep in touch and you would be coming home, or perhaps even be at home more often than if you were at a college far from home. From your standpoint you wouldn't be losing friends but expanding your circle by making some new friends.

To be successful in becoming a dancer you must be strongly oriented to that goal and willing to commit yourself every day to meeting your objectives. This may mean self-denial of some experiences that might be pleasurable and some things that you may have come to consider as necessities. That may require you becoming more self-centered and self-confident but without being egotistical.

It will also require you to be willing to accept instruction and to follow orders directed towards your self-improvement as a dancer. That doesn't mean you should always have to do so without question. You may not be used to taking orders from anyone, but you can become used to seeing if it may not be in your interest to do so. The self-disciplined person will find it easier to understand and accept discipline from others where it is necessary.

If you are entering into or already involved in the study of ballet, you will find instructions, forms and rules that may seem arbitrary or even illogical. Prescribed forms of dance or any other form of physical activity may seem artificial. If so, it may be because the action or movement may be unnatural but for the purpose of producing a desired artistic effect. By looking backward from the effect to the cause it may be easier to see why it is necessary and why it should be acceptable.

Your ability to cope will be greatly dependent on your willingness to try and to learn from experience. Benjamin Rush, a famous physician of our colonial days, said in his autobiography, "I now saw that men do not become wise by the experience of other people. Subsequent observations taught me that even our own experience does not always produce wise conduct though the lessons for that purpose are sometimes repeated two or three times." William Shippen, Jr., who lived during the same period, said, "Experience is the mother of truth; and by experience we learn wisdom."

4

GENERAL HEALTH

Most dancers think that if they can dance, they are healthy. How could they be unhealthy and still dance? Generally, it does require good health to dance. However, just because a dancer is performing doesn't mean that he or she is healthy—a dancer may be performing in spite of poor health. Dance is laden with such misattributions.

Good health does not mean that you are entirely free of any physical disorder or defect. If it did, none of us could be considered perfectly healthy. Good health refers to the absence or infrequent occurrence of illness or injury, and that when these do occur they are of a relatively minor nature with a rapid, uneventful recovery. For example, a person with a murmur due to an insufficient heart valve may enjoy good health and never have a physical problem resulting from it. Another person with a blind eye may also enjoy good health and may function normally in many living activities, including dancing, without any problem.

Chronic illness or disease, such as diabetes, asthma, epilepsy and high blood pressure, are not reasons why people who have such conditions cannot become dancers if proper controls are specified and followed. The presence of such problems may provide a person who has them with a good reason to control them carefully in order to enjoy vigorous and rewarding physical activity. This is especially true in young persons who may have a tendency to skip necessary medication. A person who has such a condition, and his or her family if still a child or adolescent, should consider carefully whether or not they can cope with it under the stress involved in undertaking a career in dance.

Visible and handicapping physical defects, such as missing fingers or an entire missing extremity, may provide an aesthetic problem, even if function for the particular dance activity may be satisfactory. Peg-Leg Bates was a successful tap dancer in show business for many years in spite of an artificial leg. His success, however, was more because of the novelty rather than his skill as a dancer. Scoliosis of the spine, which is reasonably common in adolescent females, has not prevented some of them from dance careers, but even if it is controlled can create a serious aesthetic problem in ballet.

Many children and adolescents as well as adults may not have had a general health evaluation by a physician except preparatory to school admission or for participation on a sports team unless they have had a recent major illness. Schools of dance have various requirements regarding medical examination and qualification, but this may involve nothing more than a statement from the physician that the candidate is apparently well and able to undertake the program.

All dance schools and companies should provide annual physical examinations at little or no cost to their dancers. Failing that, your family physician may be able to do this for you. If you don't have one and if the usual professional fee is a problem for you, try calling the office of your local or county medical society. They can help you to find an appropriate source at a reasonable charge.

Self-evaluation may provide a good general guide, but may overlook factors which could be important in ways that might not be familiar to the inexperienced. The medical advice in this chapter is not a substitute for medical care and treatment. It is intended to be a guide toward seeking and understanding pertinent medical concerns of dancers.

In the absence of a recent health evaluation, including a physical examination, it could be useful for the dancer to look at the questionnaire and examination form shown in exhibit 4-1. Writing down the answers to the questions and making notes about one's personal estimate of the physical findings can provide a good basis for deciding whether the performance of such an evaluation might be helpful in planning present and future dance activities.

Infectious Disease

In the personal history, having had the various childhood infectious diseases, or having been immunized successfully against them, is in your favor. When they strike you for the first time as an adolescent or adult they can make you sicker, usually for a longer time, and sometimes with lasting results. For a woman, having measles during pregnancy can cause birth defects in her unborn child. For a man, mumps can cause a severe orchitis (inflammation of the testicles) and may make him sterile. For either woman or man, mononucleosis for the first time can cause a prolonged and debilitating illness. Rheumatic fever is uncommon today compared to 30 years ago, and is probably prevented by the prompt use of antibiotics in streptococcus infections. Unrecognized and untreated, it may cause a chronic heart problem.

Asthma

A history of repeated attacks of shortness of breath accompanying exercise or with a respiratory infection suggest a tendency to asthma, even if the diagnosis has not been made by a physician. Severe constriction of the bronchial airways may occur following exercise without other symptoms of asthma at other times. In the great majority of instances this condition can be controlled by the correct use of the right medications, and sometimes with the assistance of desensitization. There is no reason why it should prevent a dancer from dancing in any category. The dancing itself may improve the affected person's ability in normal daily activities.

Convulsions

Convulsive disorders may begin early in childhood, and will sometimes disappear with maturity. They range in severity from *petit mal* (brief episodes of loss of attention without spasmodic reaction) to *grand mal* (loss of consciousness with paroxysmal chronic and tonic limb contractions). This is sometimes the result from a brain injury sustained at any period of life. The majority of these disorders may be controlled by medication if it is taken in the right quantity and on a regular basis. There is no reason why a dancer should not be able to dance effectively as long as the seizure activity is under proper control.

Heart Problems

A history of a heart murmur is not necessarily serious, particularly for a person who has not had rheumatic fever. Most of these murmurs heard in children and adolescents are functional and disappear with full growth. Having frequent irregular heartbeats or runs of very rapid beats can be serious and should be investigated by a physician. Drinking coffee very frequently and regularly, as well as heavy cigarette smoking, can be a cause of the occasional irregular beat (extra systole). Cutting down on coffee and stopping smoking will usually correct the problem. If the irregular heartbeats persist in spite of doing both, there may be some problem in the heart muscle or its conducting system. Resting and exercise electrocardiograms, and possibly an echocardiogram may confirm the diagnosis. Some irregularities can be controlled or prevented by medication. There is some chance of cardiac arrest during vigorous exercise in a person who has persistent extra systoles.

Bladder and Kidney Infections

Bladder infections (cystitis) and kidney infections (nephritis) are more common in girls than in boys. When there is a history of repeated infections, the person should be examined by a urologist and have special x-rays, urine cultures and other tests done to discover the cause and correct it if possible. Some of these causes, such as a double kidney or double ureter, may require surgical treatment to prevent chronic kidney damage or complete loss of the kidney.

Abdominal Pain

Recurring attacks of abdominal pain, with or without loose stools, requires medical investigation. Although there is no such thing as chronic appendicitis, adolescents may have recurrent attacks of acute appendicitis which are not identified correctly and don't result in a ruptured appendix or formation of an abscess. They may also have recurrent attacks of inflammation of lymph nodes lying close to the small intestine (mesenteric adenitis) which are sometimes difficult to distinguish from appendicitis. Regional enteritis, usually involving the lower end of the small intestine, should also be considered and ruled out if possible. Spasms in the large intestine (colon) are rather common in young persons, who may be subject to them when they experience a great deal of mental pressure, as in a heavy schedule of dance classes. If identified, these spasms can usually be controlled by medication, diet and counseling, allowing the person to continue dancing.

Menstruation

Menses begin ordinarily in our society in girls around age 12. In girls who have been involved in heavy dance schedules before that age they may not start until a year or two later. In a girl who doesn't have good development of her breasts and pubic hair and has not menstruated by age 16, special investigations to determine the cause should be made. Some girls who have started menstruating at the usual age may stop after entering a dance program. This doesn't mean necessarily that anything is wrong, and they may have periods when they are on a long summer vacation break. Adolescent girls and young women heavily involved in dance programs may have infrequent menses (oligomenorrhea) or may stop entirely (amenorrhea). There is great individual variation. Anyone who is having periods every 25 to 35 days may be considered to have normal menses.

Any young woman who has complete cessation of her menses for six months or more while in a dance program should have some investigation of her status by a gynecologist even though there may be nothing seriously wrong. If something is found it may be possible to correct it.

Vision

Serviceable vision is important to a dancer. Most errors of refraction, including myopia (short sightedness) and astigmatism (failure to focus), are correctable. In the majority of instances contact lenses may be worn rather than spectacles. Failure to correct visual defects can result in inability to respond to cues and direction, loss of orientation to other dancers, collisions and falls. Inability to maintain eye contact with the audience can be a serious handicap to the performing dancer.

Hearing

Serviceable hearing is essential to be able to follow music, oral direction and oral cues on stage. Some hearing defects are correctable by hearing aids which are so small that they may be contained entirely within the ear.

Teeth

Malalignment of teeth may be corrected in childhood or early adolescence not only for cosmetic reasons but to help proper nutrition. Missing teeth should be replaced. Teeth should receive frequent inspection and attention by a dental hygienist or dentist to avoid loss from cavities and the occurrence of abscesses which may cause serious disability and loss of time for a dancer.

Thyroid Disorders

Solitary swellings or nodules occur in the thyroids of adolescent as well as mature persons and are not normally of serious significance. They may be associated with overactivity of the thyroid, however, and this is manifested by a rapid pulse, excessive perspiration and often severe anxiety, the same symptoms that occur with an overactive (diffuse toxic goiter) thyroid. Both may be accompanied by unusual prominence of the eyes (exopthalmic goiter). These conditions require correction before they result in serious weight loss or heart trouble. This can be managed frequently by medication but may require surgery.

Spinal Curvature

Spinal problems that may involve adolescent and mature dancers are usually connected with excessive curvatures or pain in the lower back. Some of these are preventable and many are correctable. Some may make dancers unable to dance effectively or without serious disruptions.

Lateral curvature of the upper (dorsal) and lower (lumbar) spine may start in late childhood or early adolescence. This scoliosis may result from unequal development and strength in the muscles on one side of the trunk or from unequal development of length in one of the lower extremities (thigh and leg). The former may be arrested at a point where the deformity physically and aesthetically still permits professional development as a dancer. The latter may be prevented by early recognition of the problem and correction, or compensated later on by appropriate support. Lower back pain may occur with either type if not corrected or compensated.

The scoliosis that develops from unbalanced muscle strength tends to be progressive unless treatment by bracing, muscle stimulation or spinal fusion arrests the process. Progression doesn't stop automatically when full growth is achieved and will continue if bracing or muscle stimulation stops at that time.

Children or adolescents who have not achieved full growth may have normal growth in the thigh or leg bones arrested by injury or premature closure of the growth centers (epiphyses) of one or more of these bones. This causes tilting of the pelvic girdle to the side on which growth has been arrested. To balance the trunk and keep the head and eyes level the lumbar and dorsal spines curve. Over time these curvatures may become permanent, even when the lower extremity lengths are equalized by the use of a lift. The preventive use of a heel lift when the inequality is first noted may prevent the curvature but the use of a lift must be continued.

Hernias

Inguinal hernias occur in both males and females. Because they tend over time to descend into the scrotum in males they have a greater tendency to become irreducible or incarcerated. This leads to a greater chance of bowel obstruction or strangulation. Since most of the lifting in dance is done by males there is greater pressure on their hernias to enlarge and to become strangulated. Any dancer, male or female, who has an inguinal hernia should have it repaired prior to resuming dancing.

Femoral hernias occur in both men and women and appear below the inguinal ligament in its mid-portion. They may be painful and may also become strangulated so that they should be repaired.

Hydrocoeles are soft tissue fluid containing swellings that arise in the fibrous tissue covering of the testicle (tunica vaginalis) in males and rarely in the large outer lip (labium majus) of the female. In males these are usually found in the scrotum, closely attached to the testicle. They are often associated with an inguinal hernia and may be removed if this is repaired. Persistence of this swelling in the adolescent male should be removed, especially it if shows any tendency to enlarge since it may not be a congenital hydrocoele but a manifestation of a malignant tumor of the testicle.

Hemorrhoids

The presence of hemorrhoids may be a great handicap to a dancer because of pain or recurrent bleeding. Most minor hemorrhoids can be treated with over-the-counter medications and diet. More persistent types should be treated by injection or surgical removal.

Varicose Veins

Varicose veins occur principally in persons who have weak or defective valves in the veins of their lower extremities. They may occur in adolescence and are ordinarily not painful unless a blood clot (thrombosis) forms in the vein. They swell with activity during the day and can be painful to a dancer at night after a long day of class and rehearsal. Treatment by injection and ligation can be helpful cosmetically, give relief of discomfort and prevent the formation of blood clots, which may progress into the deep veins and cause breaking off of a clot to the heart and lungs (pulmonary embolism).

Bones and Joints

Some aspiring dancers may have problems in their hips, knees and ankles that have arisen from injuries in other activities besides dance or which are caused by anatomic variations that predispose them to injury. Problems relating to the feet are discussed in chapter 5. This chapter will not attempt to describe all the possible other problems in detail but can indicate what they may be and suggest what medical advice and help may be necessary.

Painful hip may result in the adolescent dancer from forcing turnout in the mid-teens when it has not been started earlier, as it should be. The pain may arise from injury to cartilage in the hip joint or ligaments and other soft tissues around the hip. In young males, if this pain is persistent and aggravated by even walking and running as well as dancing, investigation by an orthopedic surgeon is indicated to see if there may be a problem of slipping at the growth center in the head of the femur. Injury to the cartilage lining the hip joint can be identified by x-ray examination or bone scan and will usually heal with prolonged rest.

Snapping or clicking noises in the hip are usually more annoying than painful or disabling. It may be caused by one of the tendons rubbing across a bony prominence (greater or lesser trochanter) near the neck of the femur. Chronic strain of the groin muscles may result from lack of strength in the muscles surrounding the hip and lack of flexibility due to failure of stretching exercises. Inflammation of one of the soft tissue gliding surfaces (bursa) that surround joints and bony prominences may cause chronic and recurrent pain and is susceptible to treatment.

Knee pain may come from the kneecap (patella), injury to the supporting ligaments, injury to the shock absorbing internal cartilages (menisci), the lining hyaline cartilage attached to the bone or injury to the bone itself. To learn the exact cause it is necessary to have a medical examination, usually including other tests or examinations such as x-rays, bone scans, joint aspiration or arthroscopy, (an internal examination conducted through a telescopic device inserted through a small incision over the knee). Some of the signs and symptoms that may be associated with these conditions will be outlined to suggest to you what may be wrong and what you can do about it.

The patella is a sesamoid bone, one which lies in a tendon that rides over a joint and improves the efficiency of the muscles that cut across the joint. In this case it also provides some incidental protection for the joint. It should ride smoothly in the groove created by the two bony prominences (condyles) of the lower end of the femur. It may not do so, however, because of its shape, which is somewhat variable, or because of the angle made by the femur and leg bone (tibia), which may be greater in females, or the location of the attachment of the patellar tendon to the tibia. The variations that are possible in this patello-femoral mechanism may result in people who are vigorously active—such as dancers—in chronic strain and consequent pain. This strain may also cause damage to the lining cartilage of the patella and the bone itself (chondromalacia). More commonly this damage is minor or absent and the pain can be remedied by medication, physical therapy or surgery; thus preventing its recurrence. This requires medical consultation for diagnosis and treatment. Neglect of this condition may cause it to reach a stage where in spite of treatment it could end a dancer's career.

The supporting ligaments of the knee most commonly injured are those on the inner (medial) and outer (lateral) sides of the knee. Sprains or complete tears of these ligaments are painful and disabling. They are characterized by tenderness along the course of the ligament, loss of a full range of knee motion, loss of stability of the knee if severe, and pain on weight bearing if it is possible. Swelling of the whole joint means either an associated injury in the joint, bleeding into the joint from a tear in the ligament, or both. Medical diagnosis with recommendations for treatment is necessary. Persistent disability may follow lack of treatment for the acute injury.

Critical supporting ligaments of the knee are the two internal ones, anterior and posterior cruciate. The anterior is the more frequently injured of the two, often in conjunction with injury to one of the lateral ligaments or menisci. Failure to repair a torn anterior cruciate ligament in a dancer can terminate a career. Arthroscopic examination is indicated if this injury is suspected. Repair usually involves a major open surgery of the joint with a reinforcing graft, most commonly of the patient's own living tissues.

If the knee is chronically unstable and collapses under pressure or strain, an old untreated cruciate ligament injury may be present. Since there may be other complications, orthopedic evaluation is necessary to decide the future course of management and evaluate the potential for continuing a dance career.

Each knee has an inner (medial) and outer (lateral) meniscus and either or both may be torn, partially or completely. The injury is painful when it occurs, and usually will not allow weight bearing at first. If it is only partial the pain and swelling of the joint will subside but pain may recur on activity. This may be accompanied by sensations of clicking, catching or even locking of the joint. With a complete tear a loose piece of cartilage may move around in the joint and may lock the joint completely until it can be removed. These torn menisci do not heal themselves and the chronic state can be disabling to a dancer.

Surgical treatment is necessary to rehabilitate the knee and to prevent further damage to other hyaline cartilage and the unaffected meniscus as the result of the alteration in knee movement and weight bearing. When such surgery is needed it should be performed as soon as possible to prevent damage that cannot be repaired. Many partially torn menisci can be repaired, even through the arthroscope, and they will heal to restore normal function. The period of disability may be only a matter of weeks whereas without repair it may be much longer and the result unsatisfactory for return to good function.

Stress fractures may occur above the knee in the femur and in the tibia below. They are painful in activity but many will heal with reduced activity and not require complete cessation of dancing. Persistent failure to heal may require some type of internal fixation or bone graft.

There is no such thing as a minor sprain of the ankle, a common injury in dancing or in almost any sport. There is no common injury that is more poorly or neglectfully treated, with the result that there are many unstable ankles. An unstable ankle can be a great handicap to a dancer and is a source for frequent resprains. Every ankle sprain should be treated from the time of injury by complete rest from weight bearing for 48 hours and then by support at all times until it is healed. In this way the typical sprain can be healed sufficiently to allow normal activity with some support in about three weeks. The support may be in the form of adhesive tape or an air cast.

Dancers who have a very unstable ankle from an untreated sprain or series of resprains can have it stabilized by a rather simple reconstructive surgical repair to allow return to normal function and prevent chronic disability.

Further Self-Evaluation

Your own review of your physical assets and debits should provide you with a basis for deciding whether you are prepared, without further corrective procedures, to embark or continue on a dance career. It might also impel you to take action about something you did not thoroughly understand or were trying to put off doing something about. If so, don't look upon it as a loss but as an investment in your future.

Two other considerations that have to do with the functioning of several of the organ systems we have just reviewed are your blood pressure and the function of your heart as expressed through the electrocardiogram. You may know what your blood pressure is since it is frequently done as part of a physical evaluation, or what it has been in the past. Many factors may cause it to change and you should know what these are and what your pressure is now. The electrocardiogram can tell you a good deal about the state of health of your heart muscle as well as its potential to function normally at rest and during exercise.

Blood pressure is ordinarily measured by the application of an inflatable cuff attached to a mercury manometer. It is reported as the number of millimeters of pressure at which the pulse can first be heard through a stethoscope as the cuff is deflated over the number of millimeters at which the pulse sound begins to diminish in force and disappear. The first number is called the systolic and the second the diastolic pressure, indicating roughly the pressure when the heart is contracting (systole) and when it has relaxed (diastole). The normal ranges for a healthy adult are 90–120 (systolic) and 60–80 (diastolic) when the pressure is measured at rest in a sitting position. Lying down, these numbers would be in the lower part of the range, and standing, in the higher. During vigorous exercise the systolic pressure may go as high as 200 and the diastolic to 130.

For an otherwise healthy person there is no such thing as "low blood pressure," although that individual's pressure at rest might be 90 over 65. Persistent elevation of the diastolic pressure at rest of 100 or more is usually considered to be evidence of high blood pressure (hypertension). The systolic pressure may be anywhere in hypertension from 150 to 200 or more. Most physicians today believe that high blood pressure should be treated even though it may not be producing symptoms such as headaches because of the damage to the kidneys that may occur and the possibility of brain hemorrhage (stroke). Most cases of hypertension will respond favorably to treatment with medication, diet and a modification of lifestyle.

Hypertension won't rule out a dance career, especially if it is controlled with medication. Regular vigorous exercise may actually be beneficial to high blood pressure by improving circulatory function and providing relaxation from tension. If you have hypertension, you should be in a treatment program under the direct supervision of a physician.

If you wish to know how your blood pressure responds to exercise it should be recorded after a rest sitting or lying down for ten minutes, immediately after stopping a bout of exercise for 10–15 minutes and again five minutes after you stop exercising. Persistent elevation after you stop exercising may indicate if you are exercising regularly that you are overtrained and need more rest.

To obtain an electrocardiogram you must consult a physician who is in general or family practice or a specialist in internal medicine. It does not have to be a cardiologist, although your personal physician might choose to recommend one to you. This should be performed at rest, during exercise and immediately after exercise. The physician who examines you and supervises the exercise test will interpret the findings for you.

The tape from the electrocardiograph will show the rate and rhythm of your heart, tell you something about the force of its contractions and whether the heart muscle is apparently healthy or may have had some disease or injury. From these findings it is possible for the physician to predict with reasonable accuracy whether your heart is capable of sustaining the level of activity to which you aspire or are currently undertaking in dance. It can also serve as a guide for the prescription of any medication that might be necessary to correct any irregularity. If a person has had a previous heart problem, such as a coronary thrombosis, it can also tell something about the recovery and whether that person can resume dancing with reasonable safety.

Adjustment to Physical Problems

It is possible for a dancer to adjust to many of the physical problems cited above by changing a program, technique, adjusting lifestyle or undergoing medical treatment that might include medication, surgery or both. The process of rehabilitation might involve physical therapy, special exercises and other conditioning activity. Such adjustments may also require reevaluation of attitude, motivation and personal relationships. None of this is easy.

Personal counseling may be available and may be offered by any of those involved in helping to make this adjustment possible: physician, therapist, trainer or nurse. If none of these can satisfy the individual's needs consultation with a personal psychologist may be advisable.

Some physical problems can be addressed short term by making certain compensations for them without doing anything to correct them. This may be necessary at some time because of pressure of time, necessity of taking care of other things or people, or lack of money. It is important to a career not to allow such temporary compensations to become continuing. If they don't fail because of their inadequacy they may create additional problems of themselves.

Finally, not every serious physical problem has a practical and reasonable solution to allow a dancer to begin, continue or resume a career. The decision to change direction is a very serious one and may mean adopting an entire new way of life. It should be carefully considered and be informed by expert and experienced advice. The personal cost may be high but the cost of carrying on against the insuperable problem will be even higher.

Exhibit 4-1
Medical Qualification for
Vigorous Exercise and Dance

1. Have you ever had or do you have now?
   If you have had any of these conditions please give some specifics
   regarding your treatment, if any, and the result on the lines at the end of
   the list.

   ____ Arthritis
   ____ Asthma
   ____ Back trouble
   ____ Chest pain
   ____ Diabetes
   ____ Epilepsy
   ____ Fainting attacks
   ____ Headaches, severe
   ____ Heart trouble

   ____ Hernia or rupture
   ____ High blood pressure
   ____ Kidney trouble
   ____ Liver trouble
   ____ Stomach trouble
   ____ Broken bones
   ____ Major surgery
   ____ Prolonged illness
   ____ Serious accident

2. Have you been immunized against?

   ____ Diphtheria
   ____ Pertussis (whooping cough)
   ____ Tetanus (toxoid)
   ____ Measles (roseola)
   ____ Measles (rubella)

   ____ Poliomyelitis
   ____ Tuberculosis (BCG)
   ____ Hepatitis
   ____ Yellow fever
   ____ Small pox

3. Physical Examination:

   Height ____ ft ____ in.

   Weight _____

   Skin (scars, rashes)

   Vision: Right eye
              Left eye
              Glasses (contacts)
              Color
   Hearing: Right ear
              Left ear
   Teeth: Missing
              Dentures
   Neck: Thyroid
              Movement
   Breasts
   Blood Pressure: Resting
                   Immediately after exercise
                   Five minutes after exercise

   Lungs . . . . . . .Sounds
                      Expansion
   Heart . . . . . . .Murmurs
   Ribs . . . . .Deformity
   Spine . . . . . . .Scoliosis
                      Lordosis
   Abdomen
   Hernia . . . . . .Inguinal
                      Femoral
   Genitalia

   Rectal

   Extremities: Defects
                Varicosities

5

GENERAL BODY CARE

First impressions are important, especially for performers. Veteran dancers know that the audience's opinion is created by their first impression and confirmed by their last. Setting aside the experienced tastes of the New York balletomanes, most viewers of dance are heavily influenced by their initial impression of a dancer. Except for the most macho athletic movements or stunning pyrotechnics, most audience members are far too unaware of dance technique and movement to be expected to analyze or remember choreography.

> Several years ago one of the male dancers in my company was convinced that dance was defined by rapidly spinning multiple pirouettes and triple *tours en l'air*. Despite the protestations and horror of the director he would frequently attempt these unchoreographed maneuvers only to finish with an assortment of desperate, "Save-me-Jesus" steps that no dancer on earth, living or dead, has ever witnessed. He always seemed to be impressed with the results; the audience was always, to put it nicely, a bit puzzled; and the dancers were always sadistically amused by his antics. A less experienced dancer would have "crashed and burned" leaving a trail of smeared sweat and skin behind him. Even a football coach in the audience was left with little doubt that this was a major booboo.

Even the most inexperienced audience member can recognize these mistakes, and he bonds to that opinion like a New York dance critic. The moral of the story is that strong first and last impressions will improve even the most mediocre performance.

What makes a favorable first impression? Many factors contribute to making a good first impression. The first impression that a dancer makes on the audience is a combination of artificial features such as make-up or costume, physical characteristics and general deportment. Good grooming is an essential aspect of any professional, and a careless lack of consistent, effective hygiene is embarrassing as well as potentially unhealthy. As a performing artist you deserve the respect that is owed a professional, and this is rarely awarded to those with poor grooming habits.

Hair

Styles of cutting and dressing or arranging hair change almost as rapidly as styles in clothing. They may be affected by regulation of social or religious organizations, by occupational preferences or requirements or by military rules. Because hair style provides such a prominent identification of the individual we find popular classifications such as "long hairs," "crew cuts" and "ducktails." Since classical musicians in the past and country music players at present are known for allowing their hair to grow long, or as they may see it naturally, there is a tendency for those involved in these activities to meet such expectations.

Modern and other contemporary dancers probably display the greatest latitude in hair styles. Being a bit different and unconventional in appearance goes right along with their desire to experiment with and utilize new movement patterns and combinations. I don't think that modern dancers are as readily recognized in the way that ballerinas are. They're probably quite happy to hear that.

In classical dance there are fairly rigid rules regarding hair style and length. This is often initiated by tradition and perpetuated by the directors or choreographers. In ballet female dancers characteristically wear their hair up in a bun. It is important to keep the hair off the face and neck, and out of the eyes, so as to not disrupt the line or obscure vision. "Bunheads," as they are fondly called, pretty much look the same all over the world. Their hair and their Chaplinesque walk are easily identified in almost any public gathering. Just about the only variation in the basic style is the presence of bangs. Traditionally they're out and taboo; currently, they're in and a significant statement of individuality. It's a small consolation in an otherwise strict system.

Hair styles for male dancers probably change a good deal more than for women. Usually, the predominant style is a moderate, sculptured version of current styles with moderate length. Very long hair creates the same hazards for men, especially while turning. Rapid spotting may cause the hair to whip against the eyes and scratch the corneas. On the other hand, very fashionable haircuts, such as a spiky, punk cut, would seem anachronistic in an eighteenth century romantic ballet. Men should cut their hair in a style which is appropriate to the type of dance and roles.

In ballet, as well as dance in general, baldness or gray hair is *déclassé,* and every effort is made to compensate for these problems through hairpieces and coloring. Contemporary dance may be more lenient, but ballet tradition in this regard is quite clear: a male dancer should maintain the appearance of the young man in the prime of his virile life. This also applies to the presence of facial hair. Beards and mustaches are quite rare in dance unless it is part of a particular (usually villainous) character role. The leading male roles in most classical ballets are almost invariably late adolescent princes, and are, therefore, not exactly personified by a heavy beard, five o'clock shadow or furry chest.

This brings up the personal issue of body hair. For women this constitutes shaving their underarms and legs. Since tights are relatively see-through and leotards have a tendency to ride up during lifts, women should also shave in the bikini line area. Male dancers are generally a hairless lot. Whether this is inherited or acquired is left to the individual. In Russia it is not uncommon for a mature man playing the role of a boyish prince to shave his chest if necessary. The public may deem this practice a bit curious and whimsical, but the removal of excessive body hair is a much more common, mandatory practice in bodybuilding, swimming and cycling. So tell them to go bother these athletes about it, and leave the dancers alone.

Scalp hair grows at the rate of about 1/8 inch daily. It does not grow constantly, as nails do, but in cycles that include a resting phase. The cycles of one scalp are not synchronized; there is always some growing. Since growth of the keratin that composes the hair is so active from matrix the rate can be affected by conditions that affect the general health of the body. Hair growth is more rapid in summer. In sickness so many hairs go into a resting cycle that the hair may thin out. On the average, scalp hair may continue to grow for from two to six years, but some persons may have hair that grows many years longer to achieve lengths down to their knees. Normally a person loses from 20 to 100 hairs daily, but the matrices will generate new hairs to replace them, except where male baldness occurs and the hair follicles atrophy.

There are many myths about hair, such as that cutting or singeing hair weakens it, that shaving the head is a cause of baldness and that hair can turn gray or white suddenly as the result of anxiety or fright. There are also mistaken beliefs that frequent brushing and combing or oiling hair or applying various chemical compounds will improve hair growth. Cleanliness is good for the scalp, but excessive washing of the scalp and hair may remove too much of the natural sebaceous oil and cause temporary hair loss.

Seborrheic dermatitis is the proper name for dandruff. The amount of scaling varies with the season, usually being worse when hats are worn. Creams containing sulfur and salicylic acid have long been used to control these conditions. They are applied at night or as shampoos. Shampoos containing a suspension of selenium sulfide are commercially available and can be applied once or twice weekly. The most effective treatment for a severe problem is the application of a topical corticosteroid in a concentration of 0.5 to 1.0 percent in propylene glycol.

Hair sprays to hold hair in place can sensitize the skin and provoke an allergic dermatitis. Caution should be used in applying them to prevent inhalation, which can cause lung injury. Some hair dyes, especially henna, which is used to color hair red, may cause skin sensitivity and rash.

Skin

Your skin changes its appearance and character with age, hormones, nutrition and body composition. Not all of these factors are under your control. Skin color may reflect your emotions (pale and frightened, blushing embarrassment or red with rage), your internal temperature (flushed and warm or cold and clammy) or the oxygen content of your blood (cyanotic or blue for a low oxygen level). It may indicate a reaction to an irritant (rash), allergy (vesicles, wheals or welts) or an infection (measles). When exposed to excessive amounts of direct sunlight or ultraviolet light, light-colored skin will burn and blister as a response to the damage to the deeper layers of the skin. This damage may occur even while tanning. Friction will cause a blister or an abrasion, and repeated friction or pressure will cause a callus or a corn. How well your skin is able to respond to all these internal and external situations depends to some extent on the care that you give it.

The skin is comprised of two main layers, the epidermis and the dermis. The epidermis is stratified into five layers or strata: the stratum germinativum, stratum spinosum, stratum granulosum, stratum lucidum and stratum corneum. Most of the cells in the stratum germinativum specialize in the production and storage of a strong, durable, fibrous protein called keratin. The stratum germinativum also contains melanocytes, dark pigment-producing cells that provide natural skin color, absorb ultraviolet radiation, and make great suntans.

As more epidermal cells are produced in the stratum germinativum, the older cells are pushed up towards the surface. As they pass through each layer, the cells undergo a number of structural changes, become progressively engorged with keratin, and finally, die. Thus, the most superficial layers of cells, the stratum lucidum and stratum corneum, are composed of dead keratinized cells—the biological equivalent of petrified wood. These two layers effectively seal off the deeper layers from outside moisture and oil. These outermost layers also thicken in response to friction, and thereby form calluses.

The deeper layers of the epidermis contain about 70 percent water and the superficial layers only about 15 percent. When the water content in the outer layers falls below 10 percent, it begins to scale, slough, and crack, exposing the deeper—more sensitive—layers. Dry skin is due to a lack of water, not surface oil. Since most topical creams affect only the outer dead layers of cells, don't expect to affect the deeper layers of the skin. Many studies have confirmed the fact that all of those expensive lotions and creams do not penetrate beyond the outermost layers of the skin.

Because skin will take up water rapidly, you should apply water to it rather than a cream or ointment, which will repel water. After it has been soaked a cream may be applied to prevent further water loss. On the other hand, repeated washing with soap and water will rub off the outer cells of the cornified layer and also cause disruption. You must achieve a balance between supplying enough and avoiding too much water to keep your skin soft and healthy.

The apparent increased firmness or swelling in skin following the application of creams containing estrogen and cortico-steroids is a temporary swelling due to greater water retention in the outer layers of the skin.

When purchasing a skin care product, keep in mind a few basic guidelines:

1. Mild facial soap and plenty of warm or cool water are very effective at cleansing the skin.

2. Select hypoallergenic cosmetics and skin care products if possible.

3. Don't be fooled by exaggerated claims of rejuvenating properties.

4. Keep your skin care program simple and consistent.

Acne

Acne is a common and distressing skin condition of adolescence and young adulthood. These eruptions on the skin are due to infections of the sebaceous or oil glands of the skin. Oil glands are most abundant on the face, scalp, and the back and shoulders, where they almost always drain into the base of a hair follicle. As the sebaceous gland secretes its oily by-product, a plug may form that closes off the duct of the gland and the opening of the hair follicle. The oil or sebum is broken down into free fatty acids, which cause swelling of the follicle and surrounding skin. Later, a bacteria, such as staphylococcus, on the skin may infect the follicle and form a pustule. If the follicle and the gland are destroyed by the inflammation the area heals with the formation of a pit or scar.

Why does acne chiefly affect adolescent girls and boys? Society is justified in blaming this one on male hormones. Testosterone is the "main man" hormone responsible for stimulating the production of sebum (oil), and it is during the teen years when it first enters the scene. Acne tends to be more likely in those individuals who have excessively oily skin, or a family history of acne. Chronic cases of acne may persist, at least periodically, well into the person's twenties or thirties.

Although nothing can be done to prevent acne, it can be controlled and its lasting side effects minimized through the use of cleansers and medications. Regular use of a mild facial soap and warm water along with an alcohol-base astringent will help reduce excessive amounts of surface oils and bacteria. You should also avoid constant rubbing of the skin, the squeezing of blackheads or pustules and the use of occlusive cosmetics or skin lotions. Contrary to popular beliefs, diet has little or no effect on the cause or treatment of acne.

The antibiotic tetracycline has been used for years to fight acne bacteria. It is fairly effective, inexpensive and suitable for long-term use. It can be taken orally or applied directly to the skin along with a peeling agent.

Benzoyl peroxide has been used for more than 40 years as a peeling agent. A variety of brand names with benzoyl peroxide are available at the local drugstore. Recently, vitamin A acid (retinoic acid) has been used for treatment of chronic cystic acne. Peeling agents enlarge the ducts that drain the oil glands and thereby prevent the plugging which leads to pimples. If you have a pimple problem, it will be worth your while to see a dermatologist about a program of skin care and medical treatment.

Sweating

Reputations are earned with hard work and sweat. Ironically, this can have a bizarre twist of truth in dance. Every company has a story about some unfortunate dancer with armpits that smell like tear gas.

> One poor fellow I know started sweating profusely immediately upon hearing the first introductory bar of music before *pliés*. By the time we changed sides, he was wringing wet and a puddle was forming at this feet. He always had plenty of space at the barre to work, since most of the dancers were crammed together on the opposite side of the room. His legendary odor prompted his partners to take up a collection for a bottle of Mitchum. His unfortunate wardrobe mistress cancelled her plans to leave town.

Our society is obsessed with smelling clean. Advertisements constantly warn us that the road to success is littered with the corpses of those with B.O. and dog breath. Indeed, these ads remind us that virtually all personal, relational and occupational success is based upon fresh breath and odorless pits. At the same time we see sports ads with sexy models dripping with sweat. Good sweat, bad sweat. We're so confused that we cannot stand our own odor even when we are alone. Wow, what a sales job!

Well, it seems that there are two kinds of sweat: there's a watery salty type, and a more fatty funky variety. The watery type of sweat glands are widely distributed over the surface of the body, and play an essential role in cooling the body temperature during exercise or in warm environments. As sweat evaporates it dissipates excessive body heat through the surface skin temperature. In the process you lose lots of water and significant amounts of sodium and potassium. Although sweating helps to regulate body temperature, it also occurs as a response to fear or nervousness; flop sweat is a physiological phenomenon.

The other type of sweat glands, called apocrine sweat glands, are located in the axillas, and around the nipples and anogenital region. The fatty cellular secretions of apocrine sweat glands produce a distinct odor, and tend to encourage the growth of bacteria. Most sweat is odorless until it begins to breed bacteria. It's the bacteria that raise the big stink about sweating. Apocrine secretion is also more abundant during periods of emotional stress, such as a performance.

When exercising vigorously in a warm environment, you should drink a few glasses of water every hour. Commercial drinks claiming to be the ideal refreshment for the sweaty athlete or dancer contain salt and sugar. These may taste good, but are unnecessary, and may only increase your thirst rather than quench it. Save your money and drink good ol' H_2O. You don't need to worry about taking too much water since you will seldom take enough to replace your initial losses.

If you don't drink enough water and your ability to evaporate sweat is inhibited by a heavy or tight-fitting costume, you may have difficulty dissipating excessive body heat and could suffer from heat exhaustion and collapse. The serious complication is heat stroke, which occurs when the accumulation of sweat on the skin causes the openings of the sweat glands to swell and close, thereby stopping the process of sweating. Heat stroke is a medical emergency, and requires immediate cooling of the body by removing unnecessary clothing, applying rubbing alcohol and/or ice packs to the body, and cooling the body with fans while lying down.

Deodorants and anti-perspirants to the axilla along with the regular cleansing with anti-bacterial soaps are usually very effective in reducing excessive odor. Excessive sweating, called hyperhidrosis, is common on the palms and soles and may be treated by your physician with a 20 percent solution of aluminum chloride in ethyl alcohol. The trade name is Drysol and it is sold only on a physician's prescription. Failing this, there is a hand-held electronic device (Drionic) that can be prescribed by your physician to provide a mild electric current to cause a temporary plugging of the openings of the eccrine glands. It is used primarily in the axilla.

Protecting Your Skin

Generally, dancers don't have much time for sunbathing or much money for vacations. Nevertheless, the main problem with suntans are swim suit tan lines that are not covered by your costume. It is possible to mask these lines with make-up, but the wardrobe mistress will probably cure you of any future desires to bake in the sun.

Exposure to the direct rays of the sun may cause sunburn, freckling and, over repeated exposures, premature wrinkling and aging or skin cancer. With the advent of "fake baking" or suntanning booths it is possible to get a lineless tan in the privacy of your own rented cubicle. Although this remedies the aesthetic objections of tan lines, it does not resolve the health hazards associated with exposure to ultraviolet (UV) radiation. The damage caused to the deeper layers of the skin by UV radiation accumulates over a lifetime. UV rays destroy the skin's elastic and regenerative properties. Looking older at a younger age may be practical when you're a teenager trying to buy beer. But when you're 30 and your face looks like a hand-carved Mexican wallet, you may wish you hadn't followed the rays-to-wrinkles way. Once again, the ads tell us that tan bodies are healthier-looking, sexier and much more attractive. Sometimes I wonder if the ad agencies, dermatologists and cosmetic surgeons are in cahoots with one another.

Fortunately, the public and the medical community are finally starting to get wise. Excessive exposure to UV radiation, either natural or artificial, has resulted in as much as 300 percent increase in skin cancer in some populations. As a result more people are using chemical sun screens and limiting their exposure to UV rays.

Sunburn in the first degree produces an initial reddening that fades about 30 minutes after the initial exposure. A delayed reaction starts from three to five hours later and may increase up to 24 hours. It is ordinarily followed by some superficial peeling of the skin. A second degree burn causes blistering of the skin very quickly and burns below the superficial layer (stratum corneum). This is painful for days and heals slowly, with extensive peeling. Third degree, full thickness burns are usually caused by falling asleep in the sun without protection. They produce scarring and may require skin grafts.

Sun screens are either reflectors or absorbers. The reflectors contain opaque compounds that reflect all wave lengths of the sun's ultraviolet spectrum. They are usually bulky, greasy and wash off easily so that they need constant renewal. They are also visually unappealing unless you like white lips and nose. Sun absorbers contain chemicals, principally para-aminobenzoic acid (PABA), that absorb the particular wave lengths that do the most damage. They don't enhance tanning and may prevent it. They are best applied in the form of lotions or gels. The gels rub into the skin better and do not wash off as easily in the water. You will see a variety of sun screens of different strengths, calculated to appeal to those who are less sensitive as well as more sensitive to sun exposure. They are given a sun protection factor (SPF) which is rated numerically from 2 (almost no protection) to greater than 15 (maximum protection). Some are fortified with vitamin E, which may help protect. The lips are especially vulnerable to the sun. A special compound with a moisturizing base of wax and lanolin, which contains two powerful ultraviolet absorbers and no PABA, is available as TiScreen Face and Lip Protectant (SPF 15 +).

Other sunburn precautions include the following:

1. Avoid exposure to the sun between the hours of 10:00 A.M. to 3:00 P.M. if possible.

2. Don't be deceived by hazy and cloudy days. Ultraviolet rays from the sun penetrate the clouds.

3. Apply your sunscreen 30 minutes before exposure and cover every area that will be exposed.

4. Wear T-shirts of 50 percent cotton and 50 percent polyester material which have an SPF of 20. Use pastel colored shirts since white fabrics transmit large amounts of ultraviolet light.

5. Stay away from reflective surfaces such as water and sand. The shade of your beach umbrella won't protect you if you are exposed to sand and water outside your immediate area. Cement surfaces, fiberglass boat decks and dacron sails are also powerful reflectors.

If in spite of everything you get sunburn, aspirin or any other non-steroidal anti-inflammatory drug taken immediately after exposure may relieve swelling and pain. Cold tap water dressings four times a day may be helpful. These can be followed by an emollient such as Eucerin Lotion to prevent drying. For more severe burns proprietary ointments containing benzocaine may provide relief but may cause an allergic contact dermatitis. For the most severe sunburns the oral administration of a corticosteroid once daily for a week may be necessary.

At the other end of the temperature spectrum is cold, and the danger to your skin is frostbite. This can be a serious risk for a dancer since the most vulnerable areas are your face, fingers and toes. Where the skin is pulled tightly over cartilage as on your ears and the tip of your nose, and where the normal temperature is below central body temperature in the fingers and toes are the places that frostbite is most likely to occur. If exposure is severe and prolonged, permanent skin damage can take place and tips of fingers and toes can be lost.

Air temperature alone is not a sufficient guide to warn you about your possible exposure. For exposed skin surfaces the speed of the wind blowing across them can lower the effective temperature substantially, the wind-chill effect. This is why when riding on a snowmobile you are better off with a full clear plastic face protector attached to your helmet than a woolen face mask. Ear muffs are necessary in other situations where you do not have a helmet.

To protect your fingers wear mittens, not gloves, so that the fingers can warm each other and also enjoy some insulation from the trapped air. To protect your feet and toes you should wear wool socks and avoid tight fitting shoes or boots. The socks should extend above the tops of the shoes or boots to provide a wicking effect for the escape of moisture from perspiration.

The first sign of impending frostbite is when the exposed skin becomes insensitive. Treatment should be immediate covering and rewarming. Don't rub the area briskly since that may abrade the skin and by no means should you rub snow on it, which will only make it worse. Fingers and toes should be immersed in warm water at a temperature of 102–104° F.

Nails

Since *Homo sapiens* haven't needed claws to climb trees for a few million years, one might wonder why their distant cousins, fingernails and toenails, are still around. I can well imagine Mrs. Caveman waking up the Mr. in the middle of the night and complaining about the scratches on her legs after he just had another bad dream about running from a brontosaurus. A few eons later, the problems are still there long after the function is gone. Likewise, dancers, especially women, have plenty of problems with toenails.

Nails vary greatly among people as to their qualities and behavior. Some need only to be concerned about keeping them trimmed. Unlike hair, nails grow constantly at a rate of about 1/8 inch per week. If you lose a fingernail it will be three months before it replaces itself. Toenails grow more slowly and it will take six months to grow a great toenail. Biting your nails will increase their rate of growth. Illness and even severe emotional distress can affect your nails, causing them to develop ridges, furrows and splits. With poor nutrition they may develop transverse white bands or fall off completely.

What we commonly call the fingernail is only the nail plate, the end product of a complex structure that starts with the unfolding of epidermis to form the shallow posterior nail fold near the tip of the finger. The epithelium forms the matrix which gives rise to the nail root, the cuticle which lies over it and the nail bed. Nail cells flatten as they are converted to keratin and grow forward as the nail plate over a thin layer of epithelium which is the eponychia. The color of the nail bed comes chiefly from the underlying network of capillaries. The matrix itself, called the lunula, is colorless and is the partial ellipse you see at the base of the nail. The nail plate glides over the nail bed and its epithelium but adheres to it so strongly that when the nail is ripped off the epithelium comes with it. The plate and epithelium grow outward at the same rate, which is why when you have a small blood clot (hematoma) under the plate it grows out with it. If the clot is large enough to cause pressure and pain it should be evacuated by having a physician drill through the plate.

The nail plate lies in grooves that are shallow on each side and deep at the base. Nail folds surround these grooves and provide a pathway for the spread of infection around the base of the nail, paronychia. It is sometimes necessary to remove a portion of the plate to drain these infections and prevent them from involving the bone which lies directly beneath the matrix.

The cuticle is a major center of interest to the manicurist, who pushes it back over the lunula but must be careful not to injure the nail fold. An extension of the eponychia along the lateral fold which may be partially separated and sore is called a hangnail. It should be cut off, not pulled off, which may injure the posterior nail fold. Use of a nail cream containing glyceryl stearate, lanolin, petrolatum and beeswax (Country Lane) twice daily will help to prevent hangnails.

Brittle nails are a congenital problem for which there is no complete cure. There are two nail hardeners (DeLore Nails and Almay High Gloss Nail Guard) that will help if applied daily. Both are low in allergenic properties and can be applied directly to the plate or as a top coat over color enamel. There is also a low allergenic enamel remover which does not contain acetone and helps to prevent dryness and brittleness of the plate (Almay Nail Enamel Remover). Since the dancer's hands are highly visible and expressive it is worthwhile to give them special attention.

The principal problem with toenails is the painful intrusion of the corner of the plate into the lateral fold, usually called ingrown toenail. The corners of the nails should be supported on the tuft of flesh at the end of the toe with its rather tough skin. When the pressure of a shoe which is too short or a toe box which is too tight disturbs this relationship the lateral edge of the plate is turned down and into the nail fold. This can be avoided by cutting the nail straight across and at the same level of the tip of the tuft. It can be treated in its early stage by tucking a wisp of cotton under the lateral corner of the plate until the nail grows out. This may prevent a secondary infection.

If the ingrown nail is persistent it may be necessary to have it narrowed surgically. When this is done the narrowing must remove not only the plate but the matrix down to the bone and all the way to the base beneath the posterior nail fold. Otherwise the problem will recur.

The other toenail problem is chronic infection with the fungus of athlete's foot. When this involves the matrix of the nail the only cure is treatment with tablets of an anti-fungal agent, griseofuolvin. This should be taken under supervision of your physician. It may have to be taken for six months to clear the infection.

Posture

We tend to think of posture, if we think of it at all, in terms of standing and walking. This is quite natural because we are very proud, although perhaps not consciously so, of the fact that we alone among all living creatures have learned to stand erect and to walk. That may sound pretentious, but it is reflected in our language and our speech. We stand up for our rights, stand on principle and take certain things standing up, as well as occasionally stand at attention, but there are some things we won't stand for.

Good posture is an important factor in making a good impression, but it does not come naturally to most. Rather it has to be learned, beginning early in life. Learning and practicing correct posture is one of the best advantages of taking ballet at a young age. Bad posture is easily acquired due to changes in growth in early life and later due to functional or organic conditions. It is difficult to correct, and even when corrected may require constant attention.

Posture is not static in the way that it used to be taught to children and cadets, with head up, chin pulled in, chest out, shoulders back and arms at your side. It is dynamic functional balance in any position of your body, lying down, sitting, standing, walking or running. Anyone who can stand and walk is balanced against the force of gravity, but it may be at some cost to his or her body that will be reflected in different ways depending on how that balance is achieved. Good posture means effective and comfortable balance. Like walking, it doesn't come naturally and has to be learned. Ideas about what constitutes attractive posture change with customs and the times. Most of us have some notion about what posture is attractive under various conditions of being at rest or moving, and I think this notion depends principally on our perception of whether the individual seems comfortable and relaxed and in touch with his or her surroundings and company.

The human body is a chain of segments, head, trunk, arms and legs, composed of bones held together at joints by muscles and ligaments. It is difficult to place or to move one part independently without affecting the others. A base of support is necessary to counteract gravity in whatever position the body may be placed. For effective balance the center of gravity of each body segment should be directly over the base. Gravity tends to pull all the segments together into a straight line. If any part extends beyond the base gravity pulls it away from the midline.

Balance can be improved by broadening the base and/or lowering the center of gravity. The pull of gravity tending to disrupt the chain is resisted by the muscles and ligaments that hold the joints together and move the skeleton. To be in good balance and well coordinated we must have strong muscles and ligaments. Our posture is attractive and movement graceful when we make their job as easy as possible. Maintaining correct alignment of our bodies requires serious and repetitious practice.

To have good standing and walking posture you begin with the position of your lower spine and pelvis. The two bony prominences on the front of the hips (iliac spines) and the front of the pubic bone should form a vertical plane perpendicular to the floor when standing. This position allows a normal curvature to the spine. Your shoulders should be level and relaxed, your arms hanging easily at your sides. Your head will be centered over your shoulders with your chin parallel to the floor. The weight of your body should be slightly forward with the knees straight and your weight distributed between the base of your great toe, the outer border of your foot and your heel. The iliac spines should be in a direct plumb-line over the base of the second toe.

One problem you might have and not be aware of unless it is very pronounced or someone has drawn it to your attention is a lateral curvature of your spine (scoliosis). This is a very common problem which often appears first during early adolescence. Scoliosis may occur when one lower extremity is shorter than the other or by abnormal growth of the spine. This may not be noticed even by parents and is often missed by examining physicians.

To determine the length of your lower extremity lie on your back with the measuring tape going from the iliac spine on the front of your pelvic bone down to the lower border of the inside of your ankle bone. A difference of 3/8 inch or more is significant. When discovered in its early stage the curvature can be corrected by putting a lift inside the heel of your shoe on the short side. This should be in your street or dress shoes but is not necessary in your dance slippers.

Breathing

Everyone gets "out of breath" as a result of vigorous exercise but should be able to recover quickly. If you get this way much more easily than those you are working or dancing with, and especially if you have severe difficulty in "catching your breath" after you stop, you should see a physician about this. Asthma is relatively common among people of all ages, but a form of asthma which is often not recognized as such is almost as common. It is called "exercise induced bronchospasm." This means that the air passages into your lungs go into spasm in response to the stimulation of exercise, making it difficult to get into your lungs the additional air that you need to supply the oxygen you are using up so rapidly. This may start after you have been exercising for ten minutes or so but may not become worse until you stop. Then it may take half an hour to recover.

If you have this condition, usually called by its initials EIB, it can be helped and prevented by taking medication prescribed by your physician before you exercise. It can be in the form of a tablet or an inhaler, and depending on the severity of the condition you may need both. It is more apt to come on in cold, dry air.

Your Heart

Years ago a common heart problem in children and adolescents was damage to the heart valves and muscle from rheumatic fever. Thanks to penicillin it is uncommon today. Children who have had it and made a good recovery may still have a heart murmur but in most cases should be able to exercise or dance vigorously without damaging their heart further. Their physician can tell and advise them as to their capability.

Children born with serious heart conditions used to be disabled and most would die young. Today they can be helped and cured with surgical procedures and grow up to have children of their own. Most are able to take vigorous exercise but should be guided by the recommendations of their physician, who may be a pediatrician, heart specialist or the surgeon who operated on their heart.

Adolescents who experience runs of very rapid heart beats or irregular heart beats sometimes called "palpitations" should have examination and testing by a physician to determine if this can be controlled by medicine and how much exercise they should perform.

Diabetes

Diabetes is a condition that results when your body is unable to process your intake of sugars efficiently due to failure of some specialized gland cells in your pancreas to develop or to their loss. It is thought of today as being of two types: the first is dependent on the use of insulin, the substance that these cells produce, given by injection; the second can be controlled by management of your diet and sometimes also by tablets you can swallow. The first type is more common in young people, the second in older ones.

There is no reason why a young person with diabetes cannot exercise vigorously and dance. There have been a number of highly successful athletes who have done this as well as dancers. If you have this condition you can do it as well, but you must take your insulin regularly and learn how to regulate the amounts that you need by monitoring your blood sugar daily. This can be done with a pin prick sample of blood and a simple testing device you can use in your home or wherever you are staying.

Bowel Habits

Probably the most frequent cause of abdominal distress and pain is failure to keep your large bowel or colon properly regulated or excessive production of gas. A reason that this can be a special problem for dancers is that many of them have irregular and improper eating habits. Regular meals at reasonably regular schedules are one the best means of control. Another reason is tension, to which dancers are subject because of their heavy schedules and attempts to meet other demands on their time. Just as emotional stress can cause the muscles that move your body to tense and tighten, so does it affect the muscles of your colon. Dancers may also become dehydrated by vigorous workouts in hot studios or theaters. Although air conditioning helps to control body heat it also tends to be dehydrating as well.

Control of bowel function depends on trying to establish regularity, which does not have to involve taking stool softening or laxative medication but simply giving yourself time to relax and allow it to proceed normally at approximately the same time every day. Taking enough water or other liquids each day is very important and something that is easy to overlook.

Foot Care

To say that a dancer's career depends on the durability of his or her feet is a truism. We all know that not all dancing is performed on the feet and some takes place while the dancer is projected into the air or while kneeling, sitting or lying on the dance surface. Still the dancer has to get to and from there on the feet, and for how many other busy things the dancer needs to do every day in order to keep dancing doesn't the dancer need to have workable and efficient feet?

Because this part of the anatomy is so important and necessary for the dancer it takes the greatest strain and abuse in the course of a typical day, and is therefore the most vulnerable to injury. At the same time, many of the actions required by the different styles of dancing require positions and actions of the feet which are unnatural in the sense that they would not ordinarily be encountered in the actions of daily life, or even in many sports.

From all this it should be quite apparent that the dancer must give special attention to his or her feet as far as preparation and conditioning for the stresses to which they will be subjected, the use of techniques and other measures to protect them from injury and the best means of treating and coping with foot injuries and other problems when they occur. Major dance companies have access to specialists in care of the feet in the form of physicians, podiatrists, physical therapists or massage therapists, who can offer specific remedies to disorders of the feet. The beginning dancer and the one working in an informally organized setting or entirely alone relies typically on self-care, the advice of friends or associates and sometimes even shoe salesmen or others before seeking qualified help.

Foot Precautions

The anatomy of the foot, the mechanics of its movements and suggestions for conditioning it for the stress of dancing are discussed in other chapters of this book. Given this knowledge and the ability to put it to work, it seems reasonable to think that dancers would avoid abusing their feet when not engaged in dancing, but many do. Examples are the types of shoes that some wear away from class and the studio, or careless behavior with their feet and poorly advised and inexpertly applied self-care to their feet. It may not be easy to recall things that you do that may be harmful to your feet because they are done for the most part unconsciously. They can be divided into things that you do with and without shoes on your feet.

Probably the most common potentially harmful activity is kicking something. Kicking a ball shouldn't hurt your foot if you have the right type of shoe. But other equally hard objects have been kicked in fun or in anger with unfortunate consequences. It is seldom if ever necessary to kick anything, and by following that advice you won't have to decide what is safe to kick. You can probably kick your dog safely unless he takes offense and decides to bite back, but it's not recommended.

Another unsafe act is sticking your foot into a door that is closing to keep it open. Not all elevator doors stop and slide back and some are very powerful. A door that is being closed against you by someone else is a dangerous weapon. One young dancer from the San Francisco Ballet School was playing with friends when she jumped from a table and broke her foot. A lifetime of foot problems in one foolish *grande jeté.*

If you spend time around horses be particularly careful to watch where the horse is moving and when. A hoof on your shoe can cause much damage. If a Percheron or Clydesdale should step on your foot it might as well be an elephant. Few of you work with a circus, however, and if you do you have had to learn caution.

Possibly the most common injury to the bare foot is the stubbed toe. This accident is almost completely preventable. Jeopardizing your dance career by breaking a toe is ridiculous. Wear your shoes or slippers and watch where you are going.

Foot Self-Care

Conditions affecting your foot that you would be apt to treat yourself, at least at first, would certainly be blisters, splinters, small puncture wounds, athlete's foot, calluses, corns, soft corns, bunions and sprains. Care of the toenails was discussed earlier in this chapter. The most important thing is not to attempt more than you know how to do and not to create another problem by your treatment.

One thing that you should avoid by all means is a substance that has been a standby for supposedly protecting the skin of the feet, tincture of benzoin. This is a strong antigen that can induce a stubborn and painful skin rash. Many people who have painted it on the soles of their feet or have used it as an adherent for adhesive tape have developed a severe rash and blamed it on the tape or dye in their footwear. If you need a tape adherent there are sprays without benzoin that are effective and safe.

Blisters can be disabling if you mistreat them but will respond well to the proper care. You should never unroof a blister unless it is already infected when you get to it. After cleaning the skin with soap and water the fluid can be drained by inserting a small hollow needle through the skin near the blister and up into it. Then cover the blister with a square of white adhesive tape that extends onto the unblistered skin on all sides. This will prevent reaccumulation of fluid and a thin layer of skin will often reattach itself. You will be able to step on it without pain. If the blister is too large to do this easily, cut halfway around its edge with a fine scissor. Let the fluid out and then spray the base with a little tape adherent and replace the top of the blister and then cover with adhesive tape. Remove the roof of any infected blister completely and get help from your physician to treat the infection.

Wooden floors may generate splinters even though they are supposed to be kept sanded and waxed for dance use. Small splinters can be picked up by bare or stockinged feet and big splinters can come through dance shoes. If you have a splinter sticking into your feet try to avoid breaking it off since it may be easier to get it out if intact. If it is already broken off below the level of the skin seek qualified help for its removal. Splinters carry contamination under the skin so wash the foot thoroughly with soap and water. If a big splinter has to be removed surgically the wound should be left open to heal it. Suturing it may start an infection.

Puncture wounds from nails or other sharp pointed objects should also be cleaned and left open and protected. If the wound goes deeply through the sole of the foot and through the plantar fascia beneath the skin you should keep off it, have it elevated and be taking an antibiotic prescribed by your physician for at least two days. That may seem drastic but you can prevent a disability that might last several weeks and avoid drainage of a deep abscess.

Athlete's foot is caused by one of several funguses of the tinea class. These organisms can be found almost anywhere on the skin but they don't invade your skin until it is kept warm and damp and scaling or friction has removed the superficial horny layer of the epidermis, allowing the fungus to multiply and pave the way for secondary infection to occur. Keeping the skin of your feet clean and dry without rubbing them so briskly that you peel the skin and changing dirty socks for clean ones daily will help to prevent the fungus from taking hold. If it does, use 2 percent miconazole nitrate cream or 1 percent clortrimazole cream twice daily and sprinkle Tinactin or Desenex powder in your shoes.

Some dyes used in making shoes and stockings can cause an allergic rash of the ankles and feet that can be mistaken for athlete's foot. It is usually all over the skin of the area rather than confined chiefly to the toes and sole of the foot as tinea infections are. Getting rid of the offending clothing and use of a cortisone cream will usually clear these rashes.

Calluses result from repeated or chronic pressure on the skin, especially over bony prominences, as on the sole of the foot, over the heel and the heads of the metatarsals. Once formed they serve a protective function and should not be removed except when a complication occurs. If a callus splits the split will not heal and it may become tender and painful. The split then needs to be shaved down to its base. Splits in skin that is not thickly callused may heal if taped together. If calluses become too thick they may be thinned down with soft pumice stone, which may prevent splitting.

A corn is a localized callus over a bony prominence that is tender and painful. Shaving it off won't prevent it from recurring unless you can find a way to take pressure off that area. Trimming a corn too deeply may cause a scar that will continue to be sensitive. Sometimes it just requires a change in the style or size of the shoe to eliminate the corn.

Soft corns may develop between the toes due to pressure, especially between the fourth and fifth. These are usually painful. Amateur attempts to cut and remove them may do more harm than good. They should be given professional care.

Many dancers develop bunions, a painful swelling over the joint at the base of the great toe. This is in part due to pressure of the shoe on the great toe and in part due to the turn out of the feet. Changing to a different style shoe may help relieve it. If the condition becomes disabling because of pain, surgical correction may be necessary. This is of course a last resort for any dancer.

Minor sprains are usually treated by taping for support. Protect the skin with a clear tape adherent before taping and use a tape remover to keep from damaging the skin. Lay the tape on rather than pulling it tightly since the action of the foot may cause it to be too tight or to cut the skin at the edges.

Street Shoes

Assuming that we could live in a year-round temperate climate where it never became very cold, and that we could always be assured of standing and moving on surfaces not harmful to bare feet, and that we would never encounter objects or events that might injure unprotected feet, we might be better off if we didn't wear shoes at any time. Since none of these things are true, we should try to wear shoes that protect the feet and not hurt them. That sounds simple, but even with the best of intentions it may be difficult to do.

Heels were originally put on shoes primarily because they made standing and walking on any surface easier. Weight is more easily distributed between the heel, outside of the foot and the heads of the first and second metatarsal bones. Our feet become accustomed to the support and positioning afforded by a heel of moderate height from childhood and the structure of a normal foot adjusts itself to this over time. Walking around on the hard surfaces of floors, pavements and streets in shoes without heels, such as dance slippers or "flats," puts a strain on this adjustment and may start problems due to altered pressures and ligament strains that result in injuries. Very high and very slender heels can cause tight calf muscles and create their own problems. Dancers are poorly advised if they fail to wear shoes that support their feet properly and comfortably when they are not dancing.

Since feet come in a great variety of shapes and sizes, even though they are ordinarily in proportion to the rest of the body the only way that shoes could fit everyone comfortably would be to have them custom made. Relatively few can afford this luxury. Even if a standard last (a wooden form over which a shoe is shaped) doesn't fit your foot perfectly, it is usually possible to find one that is reasonably satisfactory. Fashion may dictate styles of shoes that very few people can wear comfortably. In spite of this it is possible to find shoes that suit your feet even if they are unfashionable.

The principal problems in fitting shoes are in the width and toe box. Small feet are seen as an aesthetic ideal and shoes that are broad are equated with "big feet." Having adequate space for your toes depends on having shoes that are large enough as well as on having shoes that are not excessively "pointed." About half of our population of all ages are wearing some type of athletic shoe most of the time, and since these shoes vary widely by brand in the ways that they fit, it is hard to offer general suggestions regarding what is potentially favorable or harmful in that type of shoe.

Dance Shoes

Unless you are involved in a form of modern dance where shoes are not worn you are going to have to learn to care for one or more of several different types of dance shoe. Even among each type you will find subtypes and there will be many different makers of these shoes, both at home and abroad. Having good shoes and caring for them properly can help a dancer at every level of performance, but there is no magic pair of "red shoes" that will make a great dancer out of a merely good one.

Ballet Slippers

These slippers are thin and flexible but provide some protection to the foot since they are made of canvas or leather. They are also close-fitting, and stretch so that they should be snug when they are bought. They should not be worn very tight for long periods, however, since this can cause poor alignment of the bones of the feet. Some dancers change their slippers from right to left to vary the pressure and prolong the wear.

Pointe Shoes

These are worn chiefly by the female ballet dancer and may be custom made for some leading dancers. They are almost inflexible in the shank and rigid in the toe. They are held in place by ribbons which the ballerina usually sews on herself to suit her wishes and covered with satin. Widths at the ball and heel vary for different lengths. They should be large enough and have sufficient depth to keep the heel from popping out. The vamp should not be of a length or shape that causes it to cut into any prominent bone on the top of the foot. A square broad toe box adds in stability much more than it loses in appearance.

Jazz Shoes

These light oxford-type shoes have a low heel, thin sole and laces. They have no reinforcement in the counter and are the next thing to dancing in bare feet.

Tap Shoes

These are more like street shoes except that they are lighter and have a more flexible sole. There is internal cushioning across the ball and the toe tap plate ends in an arc beneath the base of the toes. The tap at the heel is straight across.

Character Shoes

These shoes are sturdy since they are not supposed to have a classic handsome appearance, and may be short boots with heels as high as three-quarter inch. Women's shoes are built on a last with a wide ball and narrow heel which is stocky and may be as high as one and three-quarter inches. They have rigid shanks and firm counters and are held in place by a strap across the ankle.

Aerobic Shoes

The primary function of this shoe is to cushion the impact on the ball of the foot and the heel because of the repetitive jumping involved. It should also provide lateral stability at the heel and ball of the foot and enough strength in the shank to prevent collapsing at the mid-tarsal joint, but enough flexibility at the ball to allow good plantarflexion and dorsiflexion at the metatarsophalanged joints. The tread should be uniform to prevent unusual pressure on any of the joints in the midfoot. The shoe should be light in weight to help prevent fatigue.

Neither sneakers nor running shoes are suitable for aerobics. There are many brands with different features including wedges, cantilevers, special cushions and coils and variable widths for each length. There is one shoe, called the Nike Air Trainer®, which has been designed especially for cross training and is suitable for aerobics as well.

Fitting Shoes

Don't continue to use a dance shoe that has become heavily compacted in the inner sole or has an overworn outer sole. Resoling may still leave a shoe without enough protection for your foot.

Your shoes should fit snugly so that they move with your feet and don't slip off too easily. Don't get them too tight because your feet will swell during a day of dancing. That may cause corns, calluses or pressure sores. Always try on both shoes since your feet may be as much as one-half size different. If you have any questions that the salesperson cannot answer, consult some of the older and more experienced dancers.

6

PACING YOURSELF

Being a dancer is an all-consuming role. Studying, training and performing require an enormous amount of mental concentration and physical exertion. There is rarely enough time for anything else. Dance is never a part-time pursuit. It is too challenging, selfish and sacred to merely dabble with the technique, style and artistry. In ballet, dancers start young and matriculate into a company by the late teens; these dancers are lucky if they finish high school.

In addition to the many hours devoted to class, rehearsals and performance you may have other ongoing studies in school or at the university that require attention and time. You may have a part-time job or family responsibilities or both. In the midst of all this you may also be meeting old friends or making new ones. You budget your time not by hours but by minutes. Rest is for other people but seldom, if ever, for you.

Does it have to be this way? Yes and no. Yes, because if you wish to succeed at what you do you must take the time to do it right. Although dance may be the most important aspect of your world, it is only a part of that world, even though it affects every other aspect of it in one way or another. No, because your ability to succeed as a dancer will depend not only on your talent and willingness to work hard, but also on your ability to control and organize that talent and effort to produce the desired results. Such organization will depend greatly on your ability to regulate the time that you will devote to each of these necessary activities. Part of this regulation should be to allow adequate time for rest.

In order to make such allowances the first thing needed is a working definition of rest. One dictionary defines it as "a period of inactivity or sleep to regain one's energy." Both inactivity and sleep are important but they are not the same thing. A period of physical inactivity may be one of very active mental activity. Sleep may involve mental activity in the form of dreaming and may be discontinuous with periods of wakefulness and some physical activity during that time. The physical activity of persons sleeping varies from individual to individual and even in the same individual from night to night but is usually of brief duration and not greatly taxing.

Sleep

Some people appear to need relatively little sleep regardless of their physical activity during the day and others a great deal. This pattern may change with age. In general children sleep more than adults, and adults sleep less as they grow older until they reach old age, when they may start to sleep longer. Most people have developed a feeling for how much sleep they need by late adolescence and establish a pattern which they tend to follow unless it has to be changed due to working hours or other time constraints beyond their control. Seasonal variations of the hours of daylight have some influence. Some people, unless they are exhausted, feel that they can sleep only in hours of darkness and in darkened surroundings, whereas others can sleep in daylight and in well-lighted rooms.

There are basically two stages of sleep, REM (Rapid Eye Movement) and NREM (Non-Rapid Eye Movement). During REM sleep the eyes move very rapidly and sleep is relatively light. During NREM sleep the eyes are relatively still and sleep is deep. The two stages are called REM and NREM because of these findings. Each stage lasts roughly 90 minutes and they alternate during the person's sleeping time.

Sleep normally starts with the NREM stage with sleep becoming deepest after the first half hour. With the onset of the REM stage dreaming starts and the sleeper is more easily awakened. There may be several dreams but they are usually not remembered except for the last one before awakening. The sleeper may be very physically active during this stage, activity that is sometimes described as "tossing and turning." Most people change their position in bed many times during a long period of sleep. This second stage may end with waking up and then be followed with falling asleep for a stage of deep NREM sleep.

People may experience temporary difficulty in falling or staying asleep when they are worried about personal problems or emotionally disturbed for some reason. If you lose sleep for several nights for such reasons you can make it up another two or three nights later if the cause has been corrected. It may affect your performance on the days after you have lost sleep and you may feel drowsy during those days.

People who frequently have difficulty sleeping say that they have insomnia. That is not a condition or a disease but a state, and it may occur as a result of one of several causes. A common cause is trying to relate one's own sleep habit or pattern to that of others. People who need five or six hours of sleep compare themselves to others who need eight hours, which has come to be considered as a magic number of sleep hours, and decide that they are insomniacs. Some become so obsessed with this idea that they keep themselves in bed for eight hours whether they are sleepy or not and keep looking at a watch or clock every half hour while awake to confirm their self-made judgment. Some disorders of sleeping have a physical organic basis, and many of these can be treated when the cause is discovered.

If you have difficulty in getting to sleep or staying asleep there are some simple things you can do, or avoid, to help.

1. Try to establish a regular time each day or night for going to bed and getting up. This may be difficult if you have an irregular schedule, but it is very effective.

2. Try to find a place to sleep that is as quiet as possible. If it is not in a quiet area or surroundings try to make it as quiet for yourself as you can by closing doors or windows, shutting off fans or air conditioners if they are noisy and even using soft earplugs (Flents, for example).

3. Darkness is helpful to most people and some need it to be absolute. Try an eyeshield if light bothers you.

4. Don't get in the habit of watching TV in bed. You may fall asleep sometimes while doing this but it associates your bed with a wakeful activity. Reading in bed may help to relax you and is help-

ful for many. Don't make your bedroom a work-room if you can help it.

5. Try to have a comfortable bed. This is an individual preference. Some like a very firm and others a soft mattress. Waterbeds are great for some and just uncomfortable for others. Turn your mattress occasionally to keep from sleeping in a trough.

6. The temperature in your room and in your bed is important. Most people sleep better if the air in their room is cool, providing they are properly covered with sleepwear, sheets and blankets or both. During deep NREM sleep your body temperature falls below its daily average and you may be awakened by feeling cold. When air temperature is relatively high and you can't control it you need less covering and may be more comfortable without any nightwear. Electric blankets are not helpful for most people unless they like to sleep in very cool air.

7. What you drink and eat in the hours before retiring may be important. A glass of warm milk has been helpful to some if taken just before retiring. Alcoholic drinks can make you very sleepy but may cause sleeplessness later in the night when the alcohol has been eliminated from your blood. Eating a big meal shortly before retiring may increase REM as opposed to NREM sleep. It is better not to go to bed hungry, however. Since you may become dehydrated during sleep it is helpful to have a glass of water at your bedside if you awake feeling thirsty.

8. Finally, if you wake up and can't fall back to sleep, don't lie in bed worrying about it. Get up and do something. Go into another room, if you have one, walk around, sit down and read something in a paper or a magazine, even write a letter. Any distraction will probably help you in a

short time to be ready to go back to bed and to sleep.

Taking medication to bring and maintain sleep might be necessary at some time in your life but should be done only on the advice and prescription of your physician. There are medicines advertised and sold without prescription in drugstores and other places to help people sleep. These are all antihistamines of one kind or another. These drugs will make some people very drowsy and consequently should not be taken by them in situations where they might endanger themselves and others, such as driving a car. Others are not much affected by them. They may have some unwanted side effects, such as causing a dry mouth, temporary blurring of vision, difficulty in urination, even mental confusion that may last after the drowsiness has disappeared. In general, it is best to avoid them.

If a physician prescribes a sleeping medication for you, be sure he knows about any other medication you may be taking so that any conflict between the medication's effects can be avoided. Then take the medication only as he directs and only for the time it is necessary. Don't try taking a sleeping medication prescribed for someone else. It may be the wrong thing for you. There is probably no such thing as an addiction to a sleeping medication that is not a narcotic, but people have become habituated to sleeping medication and psychologically dependent on them.

Inactivity

The term implies a complete absence of any activity, but that's not the sense in which it is generally meant. You should think of it in terms of activity which is gentle rather then vigorous, quiet rather than busy. Relaxation and recreation are types of relative inactivity that can be restful even though they involve physical effort and movement. To describe them as not gainful would be wrong because you can gain from them the restoration of your mental and physical powers that have been diminished by other gainful efforts.

To relax physically is sometimes easier said than done. People use the word tense to describe their state of being at times. They mean chiefly to indicate their state of mind, but the use of that word reflects a physical state of tension that the observer can detect in their posture, facial muscles and the relative rigidity in their handshake or their startled reaction when they are touched. Not everyone has the ability to "let go" when they wish to or to release tension completely. Some of us feel that to do so is to let down our defenses. We may be reluctant to relax our vigilance.

Relaxation

The systems of relaxation that we read and hear about all employ basically the same principles and techniques. They emphasize conscious control of muscular tension. Typically they recommend finding a time and place to lie down comfortably in loose-fitting clothing in a quiet atmosphere, perhaps with soft music playing or to the sound of a monotonous, repetitive noise such as waves breaking gently on a shore. Beginning with the muscles in your hands or feet you direct them to release their tension and then work gradually through each muscle group in your body until all are as relaxed as possible. Your mind is supposed to occupy itself only with peaceful soothing thoughts during this time and for a few minutes after the release is complete. This process is repeated twice daily at first, and then as desired or required without a fixed schedule.

Many people find that once they have acquired the facility of relaxing by this technique they can do it at any time and under many different circumstances. Sitting at an office desk or in an easy chair in a living room, or riding as a passenger in a car or on an airplane, are examples. Although it may seem paradoxical, the ability to focus your attention and to concentrate is important in the process of relaxation. A person who is hypnotized is not asleep or unconscious, even though he or she may be unresponsive unless spoken to or commanded to do something. This is a restful and relaxed state because the person's attention is entirely concentrated on the hypnotist.

The successful athlete is able to maintain intense concentration but at the same time to feel completely relaxed. The ability to do this was probably first epitomized in the adjective "cool" which as long as a hundred years ago was used to describe a person as calmly audacious or impudent. This gave rise to the description "cool and collected," and in modern times to the street use of the adjective to describe someone who is self-controlled and detached. Although the famous baseball pitcher Satchel Paige was seldom described as being cool he knew how to relax. One of his six rules for staying young was, "Keep the juices flowing by jangling around gently as you move."

Recreation

Recreative activity can be very quiet, with relatively little physical involvement, or very vigorous and tiring. It can range from watching television or a film through reading a book, playing cards or chess, knitting or sewing, drawing or painting, sightseeing, walking, running, swimming or cycling, engaging in sports alone or with others to riding a horse or driving a car. The elements common to all of these activities to fulfill this purpose should be that they require sufficient attention to draw you away from thinking chiefly about your usual routine and that they are pleasurable.

Some require little or no advance planning and can be quite spontaneous, which is a great advantage for a person who lives a busy and demanding schedule. They have no fixed duration, don't require travel and expense and don't necessarily need the involvement of other persons. They may exercise some natural talent or skills that would otherwise be neglected. They don't need great expertise or special knowledge to be enjoyable. Others require looking ahead and considerable time and expense. These must be approached cautiously by the busy person.

If you are planning a recreational activity that is very vigorous physically, safety should be an important consideration. Every sport and vigorous exercise poses some possibility of injury. Dancers faced with the possibility of a new or recurrent injury every day don't need to add another to their list. If that type of recreation is your choice learn enough about how to perform safely and use the appropriate equipment—running shoes, not sneakers, and for riding a bicycle a helmet.

Finally, don't let the recreational activity become a major preoccupation that takes away the strength and energy you need for your dance. Can you afford to take a few days or a week to recover from an activity that is supposed to supply a release from the strenuous and demanding schedule you are required to meet every day? Keep a balance between your need to rest and to work.

7

MEDICAL CONCERNS AND AILMENTS

Urgent Care

There are a few things that you should learn to do immediately when you have incurred an injury. It may not always be convenient to do them but you should take the first opportunity because with few exceptions the longer it takes you to start them the longer it will take you to recover from the injury. Having some simple equipment always available in your dance bag or your locker is a big help. Water and probably ice in some form will be available in most places that you will be.

The first thing to do is to stop bleeding if it is present. A few packaged sterile four-by-four gauze pads applied with pressure will stop anything but a major arterial hemorrhage. If bleeding persists the pressure can be maintained with an elastic wrap.

The second thing is to apply cold in the form of ice that can be held in a plastic bag and applied over a towel placed on the skin. Instant ice plastic bags that can be activated by squeezing the compartment containing the salt (which is ammonium chloride) are good if ice isn't available. You should have one along. They will keep until used.

The third thing is to put the injured part at rest, and if possible elevate it from a dependent position. You might have to lie down and put your foot and leg up on a chair, piano stool or any convenient object that raises them above the level of your heart.

The fourth thing is compression to give support and prevent internal bleeding. A three- or four-inch wide elastic bandage is convenient, easy to carry and to use. Don't try to bear weight on an injured leg until you have a good idea of what is wrong. You may make it worse. Crutches will only rarely be available. Let others support you. For an injured wrist or arm, a scarf folded to a triangle can make a good temporary sling.

When these things have been done you must think at once about the future care of your injury. An experienced fellow dancer or a physical therapist, if you are in a company that has one available, may be able to help you to the next step. You will want to have a physician's examination of your injury and recommendation for treatment. You should, if possible, see a physician who knows and has treated dancers. In any case you should have qualified medical advice, even if it is something that you can manage yourself. If there is any question of a fracture or an injury to a joint you should have such assistance urgently, going to the office of a physician, a clinic if one is available or the emergency room of a hospital. Some qualified podiatrists work with dancers and can provide urgent and subsequent care for injuries to the feet.

Superficial contusions usually require only the local application of cold on the day of injury. Deep muscle bruises require cold, compression, elevation and medical evaluation to determine how much rest and elevation is necessary before starting active muscle stretching and contraction to preserve strength and range of motion. Return to dance depends on the severity of the bruise. Only extensive muscle damage and hemorrhage may require evacuation of blood and ligation of the bleeding vessels.

Abrasions should be cleansed gently with water, using soap if there is much dirt, and any splinters withdrawn. Dress them with vaseline gauze or with gauze that contains an antibiotic ointment, held in place with gauze bandage and compression with an elastic wrap if on an arm, leg or thigh. Complete healing time will depend on the size of the area and the depth of the abrasion.

Small lacerations may be held together with adhesive tape after bleeding is controlled and they have been flushed with water. If deeper and larger than a few inches, they should be sutured by a physician with non-absorbable sutures that will be removed some time after one or two weeks, depending on the location of the laceration.

Muscle strains should be treated at once with rest, local application of cold and compression. After the first six hours gentle stretching may be started to counteract the tendency of the muscle to contract and shorten. Your physician or physical therapist will advise you when to start isometric contractions to maintain muscle strength. Only the third degree strain, complete rupture, will require surgery to control hemorrhage and suture the muscle tissue together.

Sprains require immediate local application of cold, compression and rest. Most can be treated by continued support and early range of motion through a controlled range. Your physician will advise you which sprains demand surgical repair. A cast brace may be used for the most severe sprains. When the sprained ligaments are healed physical therapy treatments may be required for some time until normal range of motion and strength are restored.

Dislocations require urgent reduction by qualified medical personnel. Your orthopedic surgeon will advise you which require surgical repair to prevent recurrence. Subluxations need to be reduced manually by a qualified medical person if they don't reduce themselves. Subluxation of the patella is the most common of these injuries. Recurrence may be prevented by exercises to strengthen the quadriceps muscle of the thigh but surgery may eventually be necessary to relocate the patellar tendon and change the line of pull from lateral to medial.

Continuing Care

Overuse injuries require rest and the administration of medication that will relieve inflammation. Aspirin may be effective but is not well tolerated by some people, who develop stomach distress and even bleeding from prolonged use. Other comparable drugs are available, such as ibuprofen, that may be even more effective and are less apt to cause unwanted effects.

Rarely chronic inflammation of a tendon sheath and adhesions to the tendon will require surgical release. The Achilles tendon is the most common site for that type of problem. Chronic inflammation of a bursa may bring about distention with serous fluid that must be aspirated. Persistent pain and restricting adhesions around a bursa may necessitate its surgical removal.

Stress fractures need to be relieved from stress and rested for complete healing. They may not be visible on plain x-rays, but can be shown by the use of ultrasound or radioactive element imaging.

Electric bone stimulation has been used to promote healing in resistant cases.

Complete fractures must be reduced and immobilized by cast or brace until bony union occurs. Most can be reduced by manipulation but some require open surgical reduction and internal fixation with screws, pins or plates. These may have to be removed after complete healing.

Fractured hyaline cartilage may have to be replaced by open surgery, particularly if bone is attached to make an osteochondral fracture. Loose pieces of hyaline cartilage may remain in the joint and cause pain and locking of the joint, requiring removal through an arthroscope or by open surgery.

Fractured fibrocartilage in the form of a meniscus may heal and be preserved if it can be sutured and has enough blood supply. If not, the portion not attached to its supply will have to be removed. Any portion that can survive should be left in place because the removal of the entire meniscus unbalances the joint and may cause problems in the underlying bone. The fractured meniscus can be sutured, but it will be several months before the joint will be able to take stress normally.

Partial tears of the lateral ligaments of the knee will usually heal with support and rest, but it takes weeks rather than days for this to happen. Complete tears of these ligaments must be sutured to maintain correct balance and normal function. The critical ligament is the internal anterior cruciate that crosses the knee from the inside in front to the outside in back. If this is lost the knee is unstable. Although it may be able to function satisfactorily for walking and even running, it will give way in the twists of dance and cause injury to other internal structures in the knee. It can often be repaired if surgery is performed soon after the injury. Later on more complicated repair is necessary, sometimes using a portion of the tendon of the patella as a graft. Return to normal dance activity may take up to a year after such surgery, but otherwise a dancer's career would end.

Most ankle sprains may be treated successfully with support by the use of adhesive tape or an aircast or canvas ankle brace. Healing takes from three to six weeks depending on the severity of the sprain. A dancer who has had repeated ankle sprains without adequate treatment may have an ankle so unstable that a reconstruction with the use of a tendon graft to replace the lost lateral ligaments is necessary.

Stress fractures in the tarsal and metatarsal bones are difficult to detect by plain x-rays. Special films with radioactive elements injected or ultrasound imaging may be necessary. Most of these fractures will not heal if strenuous activity continues. They require protection from weight bearing with a cast initially for a period of weeks. In spite of good treatment some of these fractures will fail to unite and will require surgery.

Of injuries to the toes the most serious are those to the great toe, which bears 50 percent of the weight of the foot and must maintain flexibility in its joint. If it becomes permanently stiffened (hallux rigidus) this may be corrected by surgery, but it may end the career of a male dancer.

Drug Misuse and Abuse

A drug is any substance that when taken into the system of a living organism can modify one or more of its functions. Because people associate the word with the use of narcotics and don't think of commonly used substances such as alcohol and nicotine as drugs, we arrived recently at the supposedly non-judgmental term of "substance abuse" in place of drug abuse.

The questions raised about drug abuse and misuse among the dance population are the same questions that people sometimes ask about the population of athletes. Drug abuse and misuse is actually greater among the population at large than among athletes. The instances of abuse among prominent athletes simply get more publicity and attention. All the evidence available indicates that dancers are less prone to abusive drugs than the population at large.

This section is designed to be educational and to give the reader a comprehensive view of the whole subject of drug abuse and misuse. Many people, including representatives of the federal government, unfortunately believe that the problem can be controlled by stronger measures to prevent the importing of drugs and by putting drug sellers in jail. The only way it can be controlled is by continuing to educate people about drugs so that you decrease the number of potential customers for drug dealers. Drug testing is ineffective unless it becomes part of an educational process.

Drugs Not Used as Medicines

Alcohol has the longest history of continuous use as a drug of any that we know. Wine has generally been thought of as part of a normal diet, especially before potable water was easily available, and it has also been thought of as having medicinal value. At the same time it has been valued for its ability to relax inhibitions and bring people together for discussion and friendship. Our word *symposium* comes from the Latin word for a drinking party. Overuse is recognized in the myth of Bacchus and the rites associated with his worship. Although the chronic drunk has always been a comic figure, the decay of his health and body—particularly the effect of enlargement of his liver—have always been recognized and his life depicted as a tragedy by writers and artists alike.

There is not general agreement as to how a person can be identified as an alcoholic. Alcoholics Anonymous bases its program on being willing to admit that you have a problem and continuing commitment to change. The destructive social consequences to self, family and associates are emphasized in addition to the severe physical results.

It is probably fair to say that the use and abuse of other drugs such as cocaine has its beginning with the abuse of alcohol early in life. The gradual recognition of the alcohol user that it is a depressant rather than a stimulant leads him or her to look for another drug with which to achieve a "high." Alcohol is generally available and is relatively cheap, which makes it a starting point for many.

The active drug in tobacco is nicotine which is a powerful stimulant in very small doses but a deadly poison in a purified form in any quantity. The chief attraction of this drug as a stimulant is that it is absorbed so rapidly from the respiratory passages and the mouth that it takes only a minute to feel the "lift" that it gives. It took many years and many studies to develop convincing evidence of the damage that smoking—cigarettes in particular—does to the lungs and heart. It is cause of chronic cough, increased susceptibility to repeated infections in the throat and lungs, and the chief cause of lung cancer. Heavy smokers are more susceptible to heart attacks in early middle life, and often sudden death as a result. The main short term effect besides cough is shortness of breath because of inability to exchange air effectively.

Recent studies of people who use tobacco regularly suggest that it is addictive. Many people can stop if motivated to do so; they may gain a few pounds because they are able to taste food again. Stop smoking campaigns and programs, including the use of hypnosis, are organized around developing and maintaining motivation. Dancers should be motivated by being able to breathe with less effort, getting rid of coughing, and having greater endurance.

Marijuana is usually smoked but may be chewed or eaten. It is a depressant rather than a stimulant. It appears to be effective in preventing nausea in persons taking powerful drugs for treatment of advanced cancer.

Habituation to smoking marijuana can be as physically damaging to the lungs as tobacco. Direct association with heart attacks has not been demonstrated, but if the increased carbon monoxide in the blood of tobacco smokers is a factor there is probably a connection, since similar levels are found in marijuana smokers. The chief social result of habituation is that the person gradually loses interest and energy in doing much else beside supporting and enjoying his or her habit.

Cocaine comes from the Andean mountain region of Northwest South America. The leaf containing the drug was chewed by the natives, supposedly to provide relief from their arduous work and lives. It became a popular social drug and was legal in the nineteenth century. It was an original ingredient in Coca Cola, which took its name from the drug. In concentrated form the drug is a deadly poison, and it is currently illegally available now in a form called "crack." Its principal effect is to produce a heightened sensation or "rush" which lasts for about one minute after it has been absorbed. There is some suggestion that it brings on aggression. It certainly causes marked confusion and over time permanent brain damage. Habituation is common but it is not true addiction and there are no withdrawal symptoms.

Narcotics

Opium, which is made from a species of poppy, has a long history of use and abuse in different forms. In recent years the most common illegal form is heroin, which is often injected into a vein to get a rapid powerful effect. Drugs made from opium, especially morphine and codeine, have long been known for their ability to relieve pain, induce sleep and suppress cough in medicine. They are mainly used to induce a dream-like state. More effective narcotics such as demerol and percodan have been synthesized and are available, but morphine is still used medically.

Opium and its products are addictive and there are severe withdrawal symptoms. These may be lessened by the use of another synthetic, methadone, which serves as a replacement for opium in the treatment of addiction by gradual withdrawal and as a drug of maintenance.

Stimulants and Appetite Suppressants

Amphetamines, of which benzedrine, dexedrine and methedrine are the common forms, are potent stimulants of the brain. They have been used to promote wakefulness and to counteract the effects of sleeping medications. Their principal use in recent years has been due to their ability to suppress appetite as a means of weight reduction by the obese. Repeated and prolonged use can produce serious mental disturbances and chronic brain damage. They have been used by dancers to help keep themselves very thin as well as to counteract fatigue. Tolerance is easily established which means that the effect becomes less with the same dose. One result may be that the individual keeps increasing the dose and develops the effects of chronic abuse.

Sedatives and Tranquilizers

Barbiturates are the oldest drugs in this group. The best known is phenobarbital. It is inexpensive and effective and produces few unwanted effects. Seconal is another commonly used short acting barbiturate which may help people sleep. Habituation to barbiturates is not common today because of the many tranquilizers available.

Valium and Librium are probably the two best-known and widely used tranquilizers. Both are used to help control alcoholics who are suffering from delirium tremens. They are not very toxic except in very high doses. Habituation is common. There are no withdrawal symptoms.

Drugs to Help Performance

Drugs developed to help persons with heart problems and high blood pressure slow the heart beat down. Known as beta blockers because of their effect on the nervous control of the circulation, they have been found helpful to musical artists who suffer from performance anxiety or stage fright. Their use should be controlled by a physician. There is no evidence of their abuse by dancers.

Strength develops and is maintained under the influence of the male hormone testosterone in women as well as in men. It is not used by women for that purpose because of its virilizing effects, which are permanent.

Artificially developed synthetics whose actions mimic those of testosterone are called androgenic anabolic steroids. They have been used by men who wish to increase their strength under the mistaken impression that they will do so. There is no scientific evidence to show that these drugs by themselves will increase strength in any healthy adult male before his climacteric. All the so-called evidence cited to show this is anecdotal. One thing you can rely on is that the administration of these steroids will suppress the natural secretion of testosterone which does work to increase muscle mass and strength.

Medicinal Drugs

Misuse of medicinal drugs can result from failure to understand or follow the instructions for taking the drug—using a drug for a purpose which is not indicated, taking a drug intended for another person or taking a drug that is outdated and has lost its potency.

When you are instructed to take a drug you should take it as often and for as long as you are told. To fail to do either may mean that it won't be effective. You may have wasted your time and money and will be back where you started. Always read the label every time you take any medication.

If you experience any unusual feeling or reaction to taking a drug don't take any more of it until you have consulted your physician. Drugs may produce unexpected effects in any individual.

If your Aunt Minnie has some drug left over from an old prescription and you think that your condition is like hers, don't take the medicine. What was good for her may not be good for you. She may have stopped it because of an unfavorable reaction and neglected to get rid of it. What she had may be different from what you think.

If you have some drug left over after treatment of a pain in your back don't assume that it might also be good for a headache or a sore toe. Ask your physician what you should do.

General Principles

We live in a very drug-conscious and drug-using society. It is easy to get involved in the wrong or mistaken use of drugs but it is not always easy to avoid the consequences of what you have done. Because you may find many people in the world of dance using different drugs for different reasons don't assume that it is a necessary part of that world and you must accept it. Always insist on knowing what you are doing, why you are doing it and that whatever you are asked to do you have every right to refuse.

Of all the things that can shorten your career as a dancer a disabling injury is the most common. There are other things and circumstances that can add up to the same thing and many are unpreventable. A drug problem is entirely preventable, and it is up to you to prevent it.

Puberty

The active secretion of sex hormones begins in girls somewhere between the ages of 9 and 15 and in boys between 13 and 16. The first signs are in the development of the secondary sex characteristics, public hair, breasts and testes. Voice changes occur in both sexes but are more marked in boys. Facial hair begins to grow in boys. The onset of menstrual flow (menarche) is a rather late event in puberty for most girls.

Since girls are secreting male and female hormones, they may be bigger between the ages of 9 and 13 than boys of the same age. This makes a difference in early dance training since girls can start earlier and work more effectively. Growth is rapid in both sexes during this period. Many girls reach their maximum height by 16 years. When boys start to grow they quickly reach and surpass the height of the girls and may keep growing beyond 18 years for several more years.

Turnout, the basic attitude from which most movement in dance develops, depends on exceptional mobility in the hip joints. This depends on beginning to develop this mobility before the strong ligaments that control movement through and across the hip joint are fully developed and relatively inflexible. Since most girls start dance training earlier than boys, in general they can develop better turnout.

Menstruation

This is not the place to discuss why you menstruate or the mechanism of that process. Because dancers may develop menstrual problems that relate to what they are doing, there are some things that you should understand about why these problems occur and what you should do about them.

Although the classic conception is that menstruation occurs every 28 days that is only an average time for the interval that women experience. If it is between 25 and 35 days it can be considered regular and is probably normal as far as a woman's ability to bear children is concerned. If your interval is outside this range you should consult a physician to find out what is wrong. If you stop menstruating entirely your condition is called amenorrhea and you should also consult your physician. Don't be lulled into a sense of false security by someone telling you not to worry—that that is just what happens to dancers. That is only one of several possible reasons and you need to find out what the reason is in your case.

If you are having infrequent menstruation with intervals as long as one hundred days it may be because your body is not producing enough of the hormone progesterone. Estrogen makes the lining of your uterus (endometrium) grow and progesterone keeps it from growing too much. If it keeps growing without this periodic suppression that may lead to cancer. Your physician can provide you with tablets of progesterone and advise you how to take them to prevent that possibility.

Estrogen also helps your body absorb enough calcium from your food to keep your bones strong. When they lack calcium and become too thin (osteoporosis) they break easily. If you have amenorrhea for six months or longer your bones may have a serious deficiency of calcium. Your physician can help you prevent this by giving you estrogen tablets and a calcium supplement.

Finally, some women who have regular menstruation don't release an egg (ovulate) from an ovary around 14 days before the next menstruation. They may also have overstimulation of the endometrium. Other women ovulate but don't produce as much progesterone as they should after this happens. This sometimes happens just before they develop amenorrhea. This isn't dangerous but it may prevent you from becoming pregnant.

With this understanding you are prepared to consider why it is that irregular periods and amenorrhea may occur in dancers and what you should do about it, whether it will continue and for how long, and how it may affect your ability to become pregnant and bear children.

Physical and emotional factors, singly and together, can be responsible for developing amenorrhea when you are regularly involved in heavy training or dancing schedules that involve vigorous exercise. If these factors are solely responsible, and not others already mentioned, regular menstruation usually returns when this activity is reduced or stopped. One thing that women should remember is that even though they are amenorrheic they can still become pregnant.

The first physical factor to consider is that when you are exercising many hours a day, and probably reducing your food intake at the same time, you lose fat. Since fat plays a role in the production of estrogen it has been suggested that a critical level of fat is necessary for sufficient estrogen to start menstruation. When the percentage of body fat falls below a certain level menstruation will stop. That has not been proven yet, but there does seem to be some connection.

A second physical factor is that temporary changes in the production and maintenance of six natural hormones (testosterone, prolactin, epinephrine and norepinephrine as well as estrogen and progesterone) do occur as the result of exercise, but the levels usually return to normal a few hours later. These temporary changes could possibly upset and change the menstrual cycle. It seems likely that when dancers are exercising very strenuously over long periods of time some more than temporary changes in their manufacture of hormones may occur. For example, they may stop ovulating and lack progesterone, as was referred to above.

Probably just as important as the physical factors are the emotional factors. It was known for some time that severe psychological stress can interrupt the normal menstrual cycle. Competition for jobs and program places is no less in dance than in other athletic competition, and probably more constant. At the same time, many dancers are trying to maintain school work or a second job and even raising children. The only wonder is that they don't all develop amenorrhea.

If you do, should you stop dancing? Almost certainly not. What you should do is seek professional advice from your physician. If there is something that needs to be corrected the physician can advise you what to do. If nothing is wrong other than your low body fat or the level of stress from all your activities, these problems can be helped so that you may continue your career as a dancer. One relatively simple thing is to take a short vacation. This is usually possible even with highly organized and busy dance companies.

Sex Relations

Sexual relations between consenting adults who happen to be dancers are no different than those between persons in other walks of life. There is probably some difference among adolescents since when they are involved in dance they are usually worked so hard and supervised so closely that chances for intimate interchanges are few.

The two principal problems, as elsewhere in our society, are the risk of contracting an infection and unplanned and unwanted pregnancy. Both are preventable but not enough thought is given beforehand and action taken to insure prevention. The resulting consequences can be severely difficult for anyone but can easily terminate a dancer's career.

It is well to remember that you can't tell by looking at someone, or even from knowing them for some time, whether or not they carry a venereal infection. I will always remember a young athlete who came to me because of his gonorrhea. "I can't believe it," he said. "She was the cleanest looking girl I ever saw." If he had transmitted it to another girl she could have said the same thing about him. What this suggests is that it is a good idea to get to know as much as you can about another person, particularly their recent sexual contacts, before deciding on intercourse. This makes the "one night stand" an especially dangerous adventure. In spite of all precautions you may be fooled. Some women, especially, have acquired gonorrhea or chlamydia infection and have not had any symptoms that would lead them to know that they have it. Condoms don't provide sure protection from the spread of these infections for either men or women.

Gonorrhea can create chronic problems in both men and women in spite of penicillin. New strains that are resistant to penicillin are frequently reported and require the use of other antibiotics. Women may become sterile as the result of chronic infections involving the tubes leading into the uterus. Men can develop urethral strictures. If you feel there is any chance that you may have been infected you should seek medical treatment at once.

Herpes infections of the vulva and perineum in women can be painful and disabling. Both men and women can be carriers of the herpes virus without showing any signs of it, since it usually remains inactive unless stirred up by some exposure, an injury or another illness. Many people have developed an immunity due to exposure in childhood but cannot be sure of that and it is not a completely safe guide.

You don't hear as much about syphilis since penicillin was introduced because we don't see the late cases who die from infection of the aorta, brain and spinal cord so commonly. It hasn't disappeared, however, and you may still be at risk from intimate contact with someone who has open sores.

In an age when contraceptive medication and devices are readily available it is still not safe for a man to assume that a woman is "protected," in spite of her personal assurance, unless he knows for a fact that it is so. Although the woman has to receive the problem of undesired pregnancy, it is the man's responsibility as well to help prevent it. Some women carry condoms with them to make up for unprepared lovers, but that is merely assuming the burden rather than placing it where it belongs.

An unplanned pregnancy can end a dancer's career, although some women have survived it and continued in successful careers. It can be hard on the career of a male dancer if he has to take on the support of the mother and child and has been barely able to support himself. Both results can occur whether the pregnancy occurs in or out of wedlock.

Whether a married woman is better off in having a planned pregnancy as far as her ability to continue her career is concerned is probably debatable. A successful outcome may depend more on the reputation she established for herself as a dancer and what success she has had. The attitude of her company and her choreographer are certainly critical and should be sounded out beforehand.

The pregnancy should not have an unfavorable effect on her dancing providing she takes reasonable care of herself and doesn't gain and retain excessive weight. It is not as easy to evaluate the physical performance of dancers as athletes because you lack the types of measurement that can be made in terms of times, endurance, strength and specific skills. Many women athletes have become better performers after having one or more children than they were before.

Marriage

"Marriage is a staid and serious pleasure, and it ought to be a voluptuousness somewhat circumspect and conscientious."
Montaigne, Essays LXXIX

Not everyone would have the same idea regarding marriage, but no one perhaps has ever expressed it better. It should be joyful but at the same time serious. Commitment and responsibilities are involved. The dancer intent on making a career must realize how that commitment may affect the necessary moves, physical and otherwise, to build and maintain a career. At the same time the dancer should appreciate what marriage might do to make a career possible and to maintain it once begun. The balance will be different for each individual and each couple. There are no helpful generalities. Marriage inside or outside the profession is a question that troubles most dancers intent on a career. Those who marry early in life before they have decided on a career usually do so with non-dancers and drop out of dance or abandon career aspirations before going much farther. To many an established dancer or choreographer, marriage early in his or her career may well mean sacrificing that career to that of the established person. To many, a person within the profession at the same stage of development risks the problems that may go with two persons going to different locations and trying to adjust differing schedules and demands so that there will be time together. Marriage outside the profession raises the possibility that the non-dancer may not understand what these demands and schedules can be and cannot accept them.

"Marriage is a covenant which has nothing free but the entrance."

Montaigne, Essays LXXVII

What you get out of a marriage depends on what you put into it. To be successful, a marriage must involve sharing, of affection, ideas, feelings and respect as well as of goods and money. It means also sharing of duties and responsibilities to each other and to other concerned persons, especially to children when they are present. This inevitably means giving up some things, but also receiving others. It frequently involves compromise as a means of reconciling differences.

The source of the saying "Two can live as cheaply as one" is obscure, but it certainly did not come from a person who had been married. Money problems can destroy a marriage if they are not worked through by both parties. Strong marriages can succeed in spite of severe financial difficulties.

"A good marriage (if any there be) refuses the conditions of love and endeavors to present those of amity."

Montaigne Essays III V

A marriage based solely on physical attraction may have a struggle to succeed over the long run. It can grow into a genuine friendship between the partners without the loss of the physical aspect and that change may actually enhance it. Aging is much less apt to diminish physical appeal than change in appearance due to illness or failure to control weight. The former may not be preventable unless due to personal negligence but the latter should be with reasonable effort and care.

8

DANCE, ENERGY AND FOOD

Dancing takes energy, and energy comes from eating the right food in the right amounts. Dancers should be lean, which means that they should not carry excess weight in the form of fat. They should not be so thin that they lack the strength needed for long hours of training and performance.

Dance can be a recreation and a way to become physically fit, but it is also a performing art demanding graceful and free-flowing movement. The dancer's personal image is like that of the general public, which is of a person who is thin but does not appear starved or emaciated. Every age and every society has ideals of what is most attractive in the human form. Our society today favors a slender body in which natural male and female contours are clearly and symmetrically outlined and not obscured by excess flesh.

To create this ideal model your body needs certain amounts of three basics types of food in specific proportions to maintain the body structure and provide the energy for it to function according to your wishes and standards. This mixture may have to change periodically according to the nature and amount of your physical activity. We measure the energy potential of food substances by a unit we call a calorie, which is the amount necessary to raise the temperature of one milliliter of water to 1°C. Because this is a very small quantity we usually talk in terms of one thousand calories or one kilocalorie. For the sake of convenience in discussing diets we call it a calorie, but technically when used that way it should have a capital C.

We know that for the average person to maintain normal body functions, including normal central body temperature of around 98.6 F, there is an expenditure of about one calorie per minute, or 1440 for 24 hours. We call this your basal metabolism, and it is influenced by your age, body size and amount of body fat. Growth adds to this requirement, and therefore young lean individuals have the highest basal metabolism. To maintain one pound of body weight the average requirement is 18 calories per day, so that if a person weighs one hundred pounds the daily requirement to maintain that weight is 1800 calories. The additional need in calories depends on the nature and amount of physical activities the individual pursues.

To determine how many calories of energy are contained in the food you eat you have to know the three classes of foods have different amounts. For each gram of food carbohydrates and proteins can supply four calories, but each gram of fat supplies nine. Alcohol, a complex carbohydrate, supplies seven. Lean beef, chicken and fish consist almost entirely of protein, and eggs, milk and cheese are made up of anywhere from one-quarter to one-half protein. Fruits, vegetables, bread and cereals are almost entirely composed of carbohydrates, although some beans and cornbread contain protein. Fats come chiefly from meats and milk and cream, but you can get milk which has a low two percent or almost no (skim) fat content. There is fat in unsaturated vegetable oils such as margarine. A good balance of these foods in your everday diet appears to be 58 percent carbohydrates, 12 percent protein and 30 percent fat.

You hear a lot about the importance of vitamins—which ones and how much you need regularly and for special occasions, whether there are enough of each kind in the foods that you ordinarily eat. You need also to have certain minerals in your diet, and you need to know which ones and where these are found in foods as well. Mostly you see and read advertisements from companies who manufacture and sell vitamin and mineral supplements that you need more of these than you can get in your regular diet. You will also have some people tell you that vitamins are a source of energy, which is not true. Vitamins are essential to life, which is why they are so named, but they do not provide energy in themselves. Vitamins play a role in converting food substances into energy.

The vitamins that need to be replenished most frequently in your body since they are not stored in any considerable amounts are the B Complex vitamins such as niacin, thiamin and riboflavin and vitamin C. Vitamins A, D, E and K are essential but can be stored and are not regularly used in great amounts. The chief minerals that need to be replaced constantly are calcium, phosphorus and iron.

The others, such as copper, magnesium and zinc, are only present in your body in small quantities and are stored.

A simple, practical way to plan your diet to take all these things into account is to think about the balanced diet plan you learned in school. It is something called 4-2-4-4 because each day you should include in what you eat four servings of milk products (including milk, cheese, yogurt or ice cream), two servings of meat products, four servings of fruits and vegetables and four servings of grains (such bread, cereals and pasta).

A sample diet for a girl who weighs one hundred pounds to maintain her weight with a good balance of foods is shown in exhibit 8-1 and a sample diet for a boy weighing 137 pounds in exhibit 8-2. Lists showing the amounts of calories for specific quantities of the common foods in the four food groups are readily available to help you make your choices. Some of these lists also show calorie counts for such food combinations as chili with beans, macaroni and cheese, beef and vegetable stew and others. They will also tell you the calories in such fast foods as cheeseburgers, pizza and burritos.

of dance, the intensity of your activity and how long you are dancing. It can vary from five calories a minute for social ballroom dancing to nine calories a minute for jazz dancing. The average for ballet could be seven or eight. Multiply that by the number of hours you spend each day in class, rehearsal and performance. Then you can see where it is added to your basic requirements of 1800 or so calories how many calories you will need daily just to maintain your weight. You can compare your energy needs to those of the competitive swimmer who uses seven calories per minute and may spend four to six hours a day in the water, or to the runner who uses as many as ten calories per minute but typically runs only for two hours a day.

Exhibit 8-3 offers suggestions for the ingredients of a successful diet program. Keep records of your weight and measurements. Don't get on the scales three times a day but weigh yourself only once a week, and at the same time of day. Take your measurements when you weigh and put both on a chart that you put up where you will see it every day. You can even put up next to your chart a photograph of someone whom you envy or admire because of their success in controlling their weight.

Losing Weight

The typical woman today feels that she should lose "about five pounds." Female dancers are even more sensitive about their weight because they are constantly reminded about it by their teachers, dance directors and colleagues. If they are professionals they may have contract weights. Exhibit 8-4 shows suggested body weights for female dancers according to their heights and estimates of the number of calories needed daily to maintain that weight. If you take less calories you should lose weight. Scale weights are arbitrary because they don't take into account body fat percentage. (If it is necessary for you to know this at some point methods of obtaining it are described in chapter 2.) For practical purposes you can use the weights given here as a guide, even though there is some variation by age and within a range of + 3 pounds. Research has shown that frame sizes are not important, although height/weight tables are frequently organized into three groups based on such visual estimates.

Your program for weight reduction should begin with careful planning based on thorough knowledge of what you are going to do and how you are going to do it. You may need to consult a registered dietitian during this phase. Don't simply try to adopt someone else's program even if it has been successful for them. It may not be right for you. What you will be eating should be palatable and acceptable to you. Weight reduction should be pleasurable and not looked at as a punishment.

Reduction of your calorie intake should be gradual, not sudden, and you should not set a specific date to reach your goal, as before Christmas, since it is probably going to take more time than you think. Your body has to start burning excess fat rather than storing it and you want to avoid the feeling that it is starving and in pain from hunger. The calorie reduction should also be progressive and you should set a schedule for this reduction that is reasonable and based on your progress towards your goal.

An important part of your initial planning is to determine as accurately as possible how many calories a day you are now averaging. This may take you as long as two weeks because the daily variations can be considerable. When you have determined this set yourself a schedule for reductions that might follow the model shown in exhibit 8-5.

The following suggestions may be helpful in carrying out your program of reduction:

1. Try to eat regularly three times a day and don't skip breakfast.

2. Plan your meals around familiar foods with which you are comfortable.

3. Avoid snacking. Drink water, tea or coffee (black) or fruit juice.

4. Choose low calorie foods and season what you eat when appropriate to make it tasty.

5. When you eat meats eat only moderate amounts—three ounces of red or five ounces of white meat.

6. Don't add high calorie ingredients or dressings to your salad.

7. Use low fat dairy products.

8. Hot cereals take more time to prepare but have about the same calories as cold and are more filling.

9. You may reach a point where you are losing fat but not weight. This may be due to a cyclic retention of water which will end with excretion of the excess water in another week or two.

Dangerous and Ineffective Eating and Reducing Habits

Anorexia and bulimia are related disorders of eating behavior that frequently go together. Although they involve adolescent females for the most part, they can affect males as well. Although the anorexic becomes progressively thinner, it is not because of a lack of appetite initially that she refuses to eat. Rather she has an obsessive fear of being fat for various reasons, one of which may be that she recognizes that she has a voracious appetite. This may take control periodically in food binges followed by forced vomiting, which is the pattern of the bulimic. The bulimic may have average or above average weight, however.

The typical anorexic is a perfectionist and a high achiever with above average intelligence. She has an implacable attitude toward eating that denies hunger and absolutely ignores any advice, reassurance or threats. The factors that create this disorder are apparently multiple, including some within the individual, some in the family and some in the particular cultural environment. In spite of every effort to help them, some anorexics will continue to pursue this course until it causes their death. Very few dancers are true anorexics. Depriving yourself of food because you must to satisfy a body image associated with dance will not of itself make a person anorectic unless other factors are present. It may bring about illness or injury that is related to starvation if it is excessive.

Forced vomiting following binging and the use of diuretics to reduce weight are unfortunately practiced by some dancers who otherwise lack the self-discipline and control necessary to maintain their desired weight by better management of their diet and eating patterns. Both cause dehydration, which decreases strength and performance and can endanger the heart because of the unfavorable changes in the balance of the essential sodium and potassium ions in the body. Aspiration of vomiters can bring about lung infection and damage and may on occasion obstruct the trachea, causing suffocation.

These disorders tend to be contagious in groups of young women. The young dancer must constantly be on guard against them. They are self-punishing and inconsistent with establishing a career in which one can be satisfied and productive and take pride.

Exhibit 8-1

Breakfast:	Calories	Food Group
Corn flakes (3/4 cup)	72	Grain
Milk, 2% low fat (1/2 cup)	50	Milk
Orange juice (1/2 cup)	56	Fruit
Lunch:		
Whole wheat bread (1 slice)	55	Grain
Peanut butter (1 Tbsp)	93	Protein (meat)
Apple juice (1 cup)	117	Fruit
Dinner:		
Roast beef (3 oz)	182	Meat
Baked Potato (1)	132	Vegetable
Butter or margarine (2 tsp)	72	Milk
Tossed salad (3/4 cup)	13	Vegetable
French dressing (1 Tbsp)	66	Fruit
Ice cream (1 cup)	270	Milk
	1178	

Exhibit 8-2

Breakfast:	Calories	Food Group
Raisin bran (1 cup)	144	Grain
Milk (1 cup)	150	Milk
Toast (2 slices)	122	Grain
Butter (2 tsp)	72	Milk
Orange juice (1/2 cup)	56	Fruit
Lunch:		
Ham (3 oz)	179	Meat
Swiss cheese (1 slice)	107	Milk
Lettuce (2 leaves)	9	Vegetable
Rye bread (2 slices)	122	Grain
Apple (1)	80	Fruit
Milk (1 cup)	150	Milk
Dinner:		
Roast beef (3 oz)	182	Meat
Baked potato (1)	132	Vegetable
Sour cream (1 Tbsp)	26	Milk
Green peas (1/2 cup)	54	Vegetable
Tomato (1/2)	22	Vegetable
Tossed salad (3/4 cup)	13	Vegetable
Mayonnaise (1 Tbsp)	101	Fat
Tea with 1 tsp sugar	14	Carbohydrate
	1735	

Exhibit 8-3. Ingredients for a Successful Diet

1. Knowledge
A fundamental knowledge of the elements of good nutrition and diet will assure a healthy, sustained dietary program and help you over many of the rough spots.

2. Common Sense
A dieter must realize the fallacies of diet faddism, and that only a nutritional program which is palatable and appealing will yield successful long-term results.

3. Reasonable Expectations
Excess body fat was not accumulated overnight, so don't expect instant results. Dietary programs which claim to lose large amounts of weight in a week or two are highly misleading. Most of these losses are water weight and have little or no effect on body fat. For example, in order to lose nine pounds of body fat (31,500 calories) in one week, an average obese person would have to run a modest daily marathon (26.3 miles) plus completely abstain from eating any food. Remember, most fad diets, diet food and pills count on your endless cycle of failures and resolutions.

4. Flexibility
People who have a weight problem will always, at least potentially, have to control what they eat. The bleak prospect of a lifetime diet which denies favorite foods such as chocolate mint ice cream or chunky peanut butter or prevents you from enjoying a Christmas feast is tantamount to never starting a reducing program at all. A good nutritional program should permit these epicurian diversions, although with a certain amount of planning and restrictions.

5. Diversity
It is important to vary the type of foods on your program. Appearance, taste and consistency are essential considerations. Obviously, a steady diet of alfalfa sprouts and tofu is less exciting (therefore, more susceptible to failure) than a balanced nutritional program which includes your favorite foods.

6. Discipline
There are innumerable pitfalls awaiting the most determined dieter. Two of the most obvious are TV commercials (they know what makes you hungry and when you are most vulnerable) and friends (they are sensitive to dietary successes which may make them look weak-willed and overweight). Absolute unyielding determination along with a pinch of stoicism is your strongest counterpunch.

7. Persistence
You must make your diet program a habit which you keep long after you have lost your desired amount or reached the goal you have set for yourself. It is as easy to establish a good habit as a bad one.

Exhibit 8-4

Height (inches)	Weight (pounds)	Average daily calorie needs
60	94	1692
61	97	1746
62	100	1800
63	103	1854
64	106	1908
65	109	1962
66	112	2016
67	115	2070
68	118	2128
69	121	2182
70	124	2236
71	127	2290

Exhibit 8-5

Week	Phase	Daily calorie intake
1	Present evaluation	2000
2	Present evaluation	2000
3	First reduction	1700
4	First reduction	1700
5	Second reduction	1400
6	Second reduction	1400
7	Third reduction	1100
8	Third reduction	1100
9	Maintenance	1200
10	Maintenance	1200

This schedule assumes you have reached your goal by the end of the eighth week. If you have not, but have been losing slowly, continue the schedule of the eighth week. If you start to gain on the maintenance amount cut back the extra hundred calories. If you continue to lose on maintenance add another hundred calories every two weeks until your weight stabilizes at your goal.

9

CAUSES OF DANCE INJURIES

The injury that ends a dancer's career oftentimes has been a chronic management problem since the early stages of his or her career. Why? Occasionally, there was a breakdown in the process of treatment and rehabilitation, but more often there was a failure to determine the cause of the injury. Injuries don't just happen by accident—they are caused by one or more factors (see exhibit 9-1).

Dancers usually don't consider the possibility of injury until the reality of trauma sets in—denial is a strong human instinct. However, this lack of foresight can prove a fatal mistake to a promising career. Steps should have been taken to prevent or minimize the possibility of these injuries from occurring in the first place. Hindsight is always 20/20.

Instead, dancers ignore the fact that 95 percent of professional dancers incur a dance-related injury (with half of those injuries causing significant disability) and dance on—until the first injury (see exhibit 9-2). Then they seek medical, quasi-medical and quack advice to cure aches and ails. Delayed, ineffective or abbreviated treatment will almost certainly send some back to the injured roster.

Ineffective programs or inadequate time for rehabilitation along with a failure to assess the cause(s) of the injury will inevitably lead to reinjury. All effective injury prevention programs are based upon an analysis of the causes of injury. After successfully matriculating through the treatment (chapter 10), assessment of cause, and rehabilitation (chapter 11) phases of the cycle, you will be ready to return to dancing armed with effective injury prevention exercises, techniques and strategies (chapter 12).

The critical links in the cycle of injury are the causative factors that contribute to injury; that's where the cycle must be broken. Typically, it is not just one cause, but a cluster of causative factors which lead to a preventable injury. Elite professional dancers are likely to have more subtle, interrelated contributing factors than less advanced dancers. At this level of competition and performance they probably would have broken down long before if anything major was wrong. Nevertheless, these factors undoubtedly affect the dancer's level of technical performance and predisposition to injury. Causative factors in dance include occupational, training and technique, anatomical, biomechanical, environmental, nutritional, and psychological factors (see exhibit 9-1).

Occupational Factors

Elite dancers work in a highly pressurized, scrutinized, competitive occupation. There is a constant unrelenting impetus by teachers, staff, other dancers and the audience to exceed the previous aesthetic standards. Any treatment program which runs counter to the occupational demands and needs of the artist poses a major dilemma for the dancer. Pain and injury management of tragically short careers is the all too frequent result. Inevitably, after many years of training and a few years of performing, all dancers must eventually start new careers.

A 24-year-old male dancer* in the *corps* of one of the top ballet companies in the United States approached one of the authors in the wings of the opera house during a Sunday matinee performance of *Western Symphony*. Between his brief appearances on stage, he complained of severe pain in the middle of his shin, which prevented him from jumping. Indeed, during one entrance, his double *tours en l'air* were barely off the floor. During one of his breaks, I felt a large bony lump that was painful to touch. He reluctantly admitted to the diagnosis of a tibial stress fracture six months prior to this time. I recommended that he see his physician on Monday and consider a hiatus from dance to allow for healing. He explained to me that he was cast in the soloist role of Benvolio in Tuesday's opening night performance of *Romeo and Juliet*. It was the big break in his career. He didn't know how much of an ironic twist of

---

*In some cases, minor details in the case histories presented in this chapter have been changed in order to protect the identity of the dancer.

the truth that was. Needless to say, he never saw a physician, and went on to dance the part.

Two years later, I heard from one of his colleagues that the progressive pain and disability had become too much for him and the company. He retired from dance and now manages a retail clothing shop.

In addition to having to cope with a disabling injury, dancers are oftentimes forced, consciously or subconsciously, to resume dancing too quickly. Many union contracts permit only two weeks of rehabilitation with pay. Subsequently, the dancer must file for Workmen's Compensation or unemployment insurance. The interval between filing the claim and receiving the money frequently leaves the dancer without financial support. According to a year-long PACH survey, 75 percent of the dancers in New York were unemployed at some time during the year, had a median income of $8,714, and did not have adequate medical care services available to them.[1] One state threatened to eliminate unemployment insurance for dancers by classifying them as seasonal workers. All of these circumstances—the poor pay and pitiful medical and occupational support services—often cause the dancer to return to dancing without adequate rehabilitation, and invariably contributes to the development of chronic injuries.

Even the process of getting started in ballet may be injurious. Most female ballet dancers start serious ballet training at about age eight as compared to 12–16 for males (see exhibit 9-3). Initially, this preparation would include the development and proper execution of a complete set of barre exercises and center work during a 90-minute class. As a dancer progresses the number of classes and the level of technical difficulty would gradually increase. Eventually, the professional dancer will take six classes a week at an extremely advanced level.

More than ever before, there is an intensely competitive push among dancers, teachers and directors to develop formidable, astonishing technique at a very early age. America loves its "baby ballerinas." Most major ballet companies take almost 80 percent of their dancers from their company schools. After a few auditions and summer workshops, a 17-year-old dancer has been given a very clear idea about his or her chances of entering a major ballet company. The tremendous pressure to make it in a major company by the late teens often results in increased workloads in an effort to accelerate the development of technique. The current wave of interest in national and international ballet competitions can make the situation worse: dancers and their schools measuring themselves by their medals.

Training and Technique

Professional dancers attribute many of their injuries to improper dance technique or training. A typical weekly workload of professional and pre-professional dancers has been summarized in exhibit 9-4. There are seven common training and technique errors that contribute to dance injuries: (1) inadequate warm-up, (2) ineffective training techniques, (3) poor preseason conditioning, (4) rehearsal and performance schedules, (5) improper teaching of technique, (6) starting dance training too late and (7) the development of muscle imbalances.

Inadequate Warm-up

Many dancers claim that a shortened or absent warm-up prior to class, rehearsal or performance contributed to their injury. Yet, they were also woefully unaware of effective methods of preparing their body for dancing. Modern stretching techniques, such as the proprioceptive neuromuscular facilitation exercises (PNF for short) used in the warm-up program described in chapter 12, are rarely taught in any dance school or company. Barre exercises were never intended to replace a thorough 20–25 minute warm-up. These exercises at the beginning of class were designed to prepare and train specific muscle groups for a particular dance movement. They can be quite strenuous, and therefore are not recommended as a replacement for warming up or as therapy during the early stages of recovery from an injury.

Another common complaint was the difficulty that dancers had in keeping their muscles warm and ready during a long rehearsal when they are only active periodically. Frequently they would sit through hours of rehearsals during which they were dancing for only short bursts. In defense of the company, scheduling multiple simultaneous rehearsals can be a very complex and unpredictable task in terms of efficient use of dancers and their time. In these situations dancers should not be required to dance full-out during lengthy rehearsals, or should be given adequate warning prior to participation so that they can warm up again. Dancers counter this situation by keeping their muscles warm with leg warmers and wraps, long nylon or short plastic pants, and a variety of sweaters, scarves and head bands of dubious fashion merit. Although these garments may be permitted by the company during rehearsal, most teachers do not allow them in class because they obstruct their view of the dancer's body alignment, muscle use and line.

Ineffective Training Techniques

In order to benefit from practice, a dancer must specifically train in the technique which he or she will use in performance. For example, during one season, dancers from the San Francisco Ballet were practicing a very strict Russian technique in the classroom, but performing a neoclassical Balanchine repertoire in the evenings. There were numerous complaints about the physical strain and injuries this type of conflict causes. It would have been safer and more efficient for the dancers to be using Balanchine technique in the classroom and performance.

It takes time and proper training for the muscles to adapt to a new technique or style of dance. In some cases it may require only a few days or weeks; in others it may take years. Many styles of dance represent highly evolved techniques that require years of intense, precise training in order to develop the muscles, movements and line. I doubt that any dancer not trained at an early age in the light, buoyant steps characteristic of the Bournonville style would be able to perform that technique after only a few weeks of practice.

Poor Preseason Conditioning

In the United States most professional dancers work under a standard 32-36 union contract, which is usually divided into four eight or nine week seasons. Between seasons, a dancer must recover from the previous season and prepare for the next by taking class. Occasionally, a dancer will begin a season in poor physical condition and sustain an overuse injury during the prolonged, strenuous rehearsal schedule. Although these are relatively minor inflammations of the tendons or muscle strains, they can frequently plague the dancer throughout the remainder of the season. If these injuries are allowed to persist, they will probably reduce the length and productivity of the dancer's career.

The wise dancer plans his off-season training program to include time for recovery, recreation and training. The recovery phase involves adequate rest, relaxation and nutrition along with the possibility of medical treatment or rehabilitation exercises. Maintaining high quality nutrition and avoiding wild fluctuations in body weight (chapter 8) are extremely important factors which will optimize the recovery period and better prepare the dancer for returning to dancing. Rehabilitation or corrective (therapeutic) exercises are best performed on the floor (non-weight bearing) or in water (low weight bearing). Medical problems should be resolved at the beginning of the off-season if they cannot be treated earlier. This allows more time for healing and recovery.

Recreational activities incorporating moderate levels of cardiovascular training are recommended. Activities such as swimming, cycling and low-resistance rowing are probably the best for dancers. High impact activities such as jogging, skiing, aerobics or other jumping or running sports are not recommended for professional dancers.

> A few years ago a local professional ballerina made the front headlines of the sports page when she won a highly competitive 10 Kilometer (6.2 miles) race. The article focused upon how the dainty little dancer ran away from the rest of the women in the race. She seemed to enjoy the positive publicity that came with being a great athlete and dancer. More races, dances and articles would soon follow, and there was less and less time for her body to recover. Within a year or so, the pounding of pavement and performances had taken their toll. She retired from dancing and running with severe injuries (multiple stress fractures) to both of her legs. Who knows how much more successful she might have been if she scheduled her training and recovery periods more effectively?

At some time during the off-season, the dancer should gradually resume daily dance classes. When he or she starts depends upon the need to recover from an injury. If not injured, the dancer may wish to continue taking classes. This is a good opportunity to work on fundamental technique at the barre and center. Whether he or she is recovering from injury or not, extreme levels of inactivity or overexertion should be avoided during the off-season.

Scheduling of Rehearsals and Performances

The tendency in certain ballet companies has been to reduce the amount of rehearsal time and increase the number of performances, or to have both occurring at the same time. For these companies, rehearsals represent the absence of income from performances and an obligation to pay dancers to practice. Since American dancers are paid by the company for only 32–36 weeks per year, companies frequently attempt to schedule performances on as many weeks as possible, and decrease the number of rehearsal weeks. As a result dancers often end up rehearsing for six hours during the day and dancing in a production that night. Ten hour workdays this early in the season can put a lot of stress on a dancer's body.

For the dancer who is returning from a long vacation to a strenuous rehearsal and performance schedule, this situation may cause overuse injuries very early in the season. Unfortunately, there is not much time to recover from these injuries during the season without increasing the dancer's chances of losing his or her dancing roles or even job. Eliminating this scheduling dilemma is really an issue for the dancer's representative or union to resolve. Companies are usually quite sensitive to the situation because it involves money and cash flow. Probably the most effective approach for the dancers— short of striking—is to demonstrate to the management the potential savings to them in health insurance premiums, Workmen's Compensation, recruitment costs for new dancers, additional rehearsal time and—most importantly—lost talent. Dance companies, like all businesses, respond well to the bottom line.

Improper Performance and Teaching of Technique

Dancers are always concerned with the development, maintenance and improvement of their technique. Nevertheless, mistakes do happen—consciously or subconsciously: the male dancer who lifts his partner without sufficient upper body and abdominal strength or the budding ballerina doing a *fouetté rond de jambe en tournant* (see Glossary of Dance Terms) before its time. Developing good dance technique takes time, concentration, dedication and lots of hard work. There is also no substitute for a well-trained teacher who understands the relationship between the body's response to training and the ability to correctly learn and perform a dance movement.

When you learn a new step, the muscles and nervous system need plenty of practice to learn the complex sequence of motor events which result in the final accurate performance of the movement. Some dancers learn new steps very quickly, others have to rehearse it over and over again until it is "in their body." When a specific movement pattern or step is practiced enough, it becomes a conditioned reflex which allows for consistent duplication of the step without much conscious awareness.

Simple and conditioned reflexes form the basis for all motor (i.e., muscle) movement. Basic conditioned reflexes may also aid in learning the more sophisticated conditioned reflexes involved in more complex motor movements. For example, the well-rehearsed basic movements (i.e., conditioned reflexes) of the *plié* in fourth position and *relevé passé* provide the fundamental building blocks for the correct performance of a *pirouette*. The better the basic foundation the easier it is to learn the new, more complex, step. All of this takes time and a stepwise progression of learning and practicing both the individual elements and the actual movement pattern. To paraphrase a famous wine commercial, "There can be no dance until its time."

Are some dance styles more hazardous than others? Although there is little scientific evidence to indicate the safety of any one technique over another, this doesn't stop the dance community from having intense and sometimes unqualified opinions about the hazards of the various styles. Over the years the School of the American Ballet has taken more than its fair share of criticism about its potential hazards.

The technique taught at the School of American Ballet and performed in the New York City Ballet requires great speed and lightness during jumping movements. In rapid *petit allegro* combinations, it can be very difficult to get the heels down during the *plié*. The failure to let the heels contact the floor and bear weight during the *plié* portion of jumping does contribute to injuries. Landing in jumps with the heels off the floor does allow for a quicker rebound, but that speed is at the expense of the foot. Under these conditions, the foot cannot absorb the shock of landing, and the impact is transmitted to the muscles, tendons and bones of the feet and legs. Over a long period of time and numerous faulty *pliés*, the dancer will develop tight calf muscles, which makes it even more difficult to get the heels down. In this context SAB technique may be potentially injurious to the dancer who cannot perform it without keeping the heels down in the *plié*.

Intensive stretching exercises along with correcting the technical problem can prevent the development of tight calf muscles. These exercises usually have to be performed outside of class, since the calf muscles are not specifically stretched during a ballet class because the foot is usually pointed whenever it is off the floor. Effective stretching exercises for tight calf muscles are demonstrated in chapter 12. If a dancer has high arched feet along with tight calf muscles, and faulty technique, he or she has a very high risk of incurring a foot or leg injury. In this case getting those heels down when landing and stretching the calf muscles is the only salvation.

For those dancers who have been trained in a particular technique from an early age with a reasonable physical facility and who continue to perform in that style, the risks are probably similar to other styles. Of course, most dancers don't have such a pure pedigree. They often represent an amalgamation of techniques, physiques, training and choreographic styles.

There are also directors, choreographers and teachers who simply don't care about the hazards of their beloved technique or style, always pointing to examples of famous survivors. Although most of the teachers of professional dancers have a good knowledge of basic technique, they do not always understand or compensate for the physical limitations of their students. Some teachers tend to interpret technique as an absolute which does not allow for an imperfect instrument (i.e., the body). They suggest that if a dancer does not have a perfect body for dance, he or she should select another career. Teachers should remember that many great artists had some physical limitations and technical faults, yet ballet has survived and continues to progress.

Naturally, dancers will try to compensate in order to achieve the appearance of good technique. Oftentimes this is to the detriment of their bodies. The forcing of turn-out from the knees and feet rather than the hips is the most flagrant example of violating physical limitations for the sake of technique. Usually dancers put resin on their slippers, place their feet in an extreme (180°) turned-out position while in *demi-plié*, and slowly straighten the knees. The sticky resin keeps the feet turned out, despite the efforts of the hips and knees to turn them inward. This opposition of forces is extremely stressful on the inner aspect of the knees, foot and ankles, and indirectly affects the lower spine. Of course, as soon as the dancer lifts his artificially rotated extremity off the floor, it naturally turns inward. Turn-out originates at the hip joint with the result being the external rotation of the thigh, leg and foot. A dancer should develop the strength and range of motion in the hip through corrective exercises (see chapter 12) and then use the turn-out he or she has and not fake it by forcing it.

Starting Dance Training Too Late

In America men tend to start classical dance training at a later age than they do in Europe or Russia, where dance is a more respected profession for men. This impression about dance as a profession as well as the late starting age for men seems to be changing in America. However, it is not uncommon for men to have started as late as the age of 16 (see exhibit 9-3). This is almost eight years later than female dancers. As a result of this late start beginning male dancers frequently take an extraordinary amount of classes in an effort to compensate (see exhibit 9-4). In their rush for technique (and especially the big "tricks"), accidents are bound to happen.

> A 17-year-old male beginning ballet student was practicing some new leaps he had learned in intermediate jazz class. He had just finished 2¹/₂ hours of class that morning. While coming down from a jump, he landed on the outside of his right foot, and a loud snapping noise was heard by one of the authors, who was about 50 feet away. There was immediate swelling midway along the outer edge of the foot. After ice was applied, the student was taken to the emergency room. X-rays indicated a specific type of fracture at a point of attachment of a tendon to the bone. During the errant landing, the over-stressed tendon had pulled off a chunk of bone. However, this came as no surprise to the young man; he had known the diagnosis at the moment of injury. He had had the same fracture a year before under similar circumstances, but on the other foot.

Excessive training, combined with fatigue, unsupervised rehearsals and attempting steps beyond the individual's level of technical ability, significantly predispose the dancer to injuries in the early stages of training.

Development of Muscle Imbalances

A well-balanced ballet class emphasizes movement in all directions—right, left, up, down, and turning. As a result, good training will develop the muscles of the lower extremities symmetrically and proportionally. However, in some instances excessive training and improper technique may cause imbalances of certain muscle groups. Muscle balance refers to the strength and flexibility of opposing muscles relative to one another. A simple example of a muscle imbalance is a tight hamstring muscle on the back of the thigh. Tight hamstrings affect the way you touch your toes and the way you walk and the hamstrings' vulnerability to injury.

In ballet the hip and calf muscles are the most common sites for muscle imbalances. Specifically, the external rotator muscles used in turning out become too tight. This tightness will restrict the amount of external rotation and thereby limit ability to turn out, a fundamental precept of ballet technique. Attempts to compensate or perform ballet steps with this poor alignment may result in injuries of the hip, knee, ankle and foot.

Tight calf muscles, specifically the gastrocnemius and soleus, decrease the shock-absorbing capacity of the foot during jumps and limit the depth of the *plié*. The detailed biomechanics of these muscle imbalances are discussed in the section on biomechanical factors.

Anatomical Factors

The dancer's dilemma is the imperfect body in the perfect art. Many dancers complain that ballet technique poses "unnatural" positions and movements and therefore stresses the body. Anyone who has ever attempted taking a ballet class knows of this frustrating and sometimes painful struggle. As the dancer ascends to the highest levels there is progressively less tolerance of anatomical or aesthetic variations. In the general dance population anatomical factors are more likely to contribute to an injury than in highly selected pre-professional and professional dancers. By the time dancers reach this level anatomical factors have long since sorted out the meek, frail and physically unsuitable.

Anatomical factors do play a role in the injuries of professional dancers, but they are more likely to be more subtle and supplementary to other factors, such as overwork and technique, than they are in the general dance population. On rare occasions an elite dancer may have a leg length difference, scoliosis, or excessive external rotation of the leg (tibial torsion), and this often has serious implications on the proper performance of technique and the possibility of injury.

There are seven major anatomical factors which influence the dancer's proper performance of ballet technique and thereby increase his or her chances of injury: (1) body type, (2) misalignment of the knees, (3) torsion of the thigh, (4) torsion of the leg, (5) inability to point the foot and (6) foot development and type.

Body Type

Currently, the aesthetically "ideal" body type in many major professional ballet companies in the United States is comprised of long lean lines formed by a long neck and limbs, short torso and relatively small head (see exhibit 9-5). Dancers with this somatotype were the favorite of the late George Balanchine, director of the New York City Ballet, and are therefore often referred to by other dancers as having a "Balanchine body." Other characteristics of the Balanchine dancer include an ability for excellent turn-out, a high-arched foot capable of overarching *en pointe* and a lean androgynous appearance.

Although this type of body may be aesthetically favored in certain companies, it is not necessarily the most durable anatomical framework for dancing. For example, in arabesque the extended leg can apply relatively strong leverage to the lower back. A short torso along with weak abdominal muscles may not be able to compensate for these forces, especially when the leg is in a high *arabesque* (see exhibit 9-5). Indeed, dancers with these body proportions have about an 8–12 percent risk of developing low back pain.

Misalignment of the Knees

Whether a person is knock-kneed or bow-legged is determined by the angle the thigh bone (femur) makes with the pelvis at the hip joint. Smaller angles ($< 125°$) are characteristic of knock-kneed (genu valgus) individuals and larger angles ($> 125°$) are typical of bow-legged (genu varus) people. Knee alignment is also affected by the width of the pelvis. A wider type of pelvis is more common in women, which results in a tendency to have knock-knees. This knock-kneed alignment may lead to problems with the kneecap (patella), medial knee strain and excessive rolling inward on the arch of the foot. Rolling-in may in turn cause a variety of injuries to the sole of the foot (plantar fascitis), the tendons around the ankles and shin splints. Rolling-in also twists the leg inward and strains the inner aspect of the knee. Men usually have a narrower pelvis and a bow-legged alignment. Of the two types of alignments, a slightly bow-legged may be less of a potential hazard and is somewhat aesthetically favored in ballet, because it creates a wider opening or separation of the legs during *petite batterie*.

Slight hyperextension (or "sway-backed") of the knees (genu recurvatum) is also common in ballet. It may also help the line of the extended leg. However, it may cause the dancer to stand with the weight distributed primarily over the heels, the pelvis tilted forward and the lower back swayed (hyperlordosis). This may result in low back pain. Improper structural alignment of this type will also cause problems in the correct performance of basic ballet technique and the development of technique-related injuries. For example, when *en pointe* a female dancer with genu recurvatum may have difficulty maintaining her body weight over her foot (i.e., "pulling off" *pointe*). This poor alignment overstresses the muscles that point the foot and may lead to an inflammation of their tendons. A dancer can compensate for hyperextended knee by not fully straightening the leg, pulling up in the thigh and keeping the weight slightly forward.

Torsion of the Thigh

The thigh or femur has a certain degree of either outward or inward twist (torsion) which can either help or hinder a dancer's turnout. Most people have femurs that are slightly twisted inward (femoral anteversion). If the femurs are twisted inward too much, the kneecaps face towards each other and the individual has a "pigeon-toed" walk. This bony variation is anathema in ballet because of the demand for extreme turn-out; switching to a different type of dance would be recommended.

People who have a natural outward twist to the femur (femoral retroversion) tend to walk "duck-footed" and are naturally turned out. In dancers it is not always easy to tell if this type of gait is a fortuitous genetic windfall or an occupational affectation.

Although heredity and normal skeletal development affect the amount of twist of the femurs, ballet training does not change the amount of outward twist to the femurs, especially after the age of 12. Students who start younger tend to have better turn-out, although we are not exactly certain why. Perhaps early training minimizes some of the normally-occurring inward twisting of the femur and increases the amount of laxity in the hip and knee joints.

Torsion of the Leg

Normally, the leg or tibia has a slight outward twist (about 12°) along its length. A little bit more than the normal amount of outward torsion would actually be favorable in ballet. An excessive amount of outward torsion of the leg (>20°) may result in patellar, knee and foot disorders, because the dancer cannot align the knees over the toes during the *plié*. These dancers look like they have good turn-out, but it is impossible for them to achieve good alignment in the basic ballet positions.

A "pigeon-toed" gait can also be characteristic of too much inward torsion of the leg (<10°). This inward alignment of the leg is contrary to the need for extreme turn-out in ballet movements. Individuals with this condition should consider other forms of dance.

Inability to Point the Foot

The inability to fully point (plantarflex) the foot due to a bony limitation at the ankle joint is virtually an unemployable condition in a professional ballet company. The strongly pointed, if not over-arched, foot is an essential element in the aesthetic and technique of ballet (see exhibit 9-6). With limited point female dancers cannot reach the complete *en pointe* position and men cannot obtain *demi-pointe*—essential positions in the performance of most ballet movements. A limited ability to point the foot may be due to bony impingement in the back of the ankle joint, just in front of the Achilles tendon. This impingement may also cause an inflammation of the tendons passing through the inner aspect of the ankle (tarsal tunnel syndrome).

Foot Development and Types

The development of the bones of the foot is also a consideration in the causes of injuries in young female dancers. Dance teachers should be aware of the anatomical, technical and legal implications of starting a female dancer *en pointe* too early. Pointe work should not be permitted prior to the age of ten years and should be strictly limited to a gradually progressive series of barre exercises between the ages of 10–12. Because of the possibility of compression injuries to the growth plates of the long bone of the toes and feet, radiographs (x-rays) of the feet should be taken if there is any question as to the skeletal maturity, especially of the first and second metatarsals and digits. The level of technique and overall musculoskeletal maturity are additional factors when considering the proper age to start *pointe* work. As long as the dancer is learning and practicing good ballet technique, a one- or two-year delay in starting full-time *pointe* work should not be a detriment to his or her dance career.

> An 11-year-old girl of Indian descent was referred to one of the authors by her dance teacher and physician to determine if she should begin *pointe* work. Prior physical examination revealed an intelligent, healthy prepubescent female of normal height and weight for her age. She had severe flat feet and large bunions on both feet. X-rays confirmed these observations and indicated that the growth zones in the bones of the feet were still quite active. After review of the medical evidence, discussions with the teacher, the dancer and her mother (who had the same foot type as her daughter), and observing the girl in ballet class, it was unanimously decided to omit *pointe* work as part of her ballet training. Although naturally disappointed, the young girl was satisfied that a concerted effort was made to determine the short- and long-term effects of *pointe* work on her feet. She is now a pre-law student at a state university and enjoys participation in ballet as recreation.

There are three basic shapes of feet which affect the dancer's ability to stand *en pointe*—Greek, Egyptian and common. In the Greek foot type the second toe is the longest. *En pointe* the second toe tends to curl in order to make it the same length as the big toe. This situation may result in a hammer-toe deformity of the second toe or depression of the head of the second metatarsal on the ball of the foot. Usually this doesn't adversely affect dancing.

The most dangerous foot type for the female dancer is the Egyptian type in which the big toe is the longest. The extreme stresses of dancing *en pointe* may trigger the development of bunions and fractures of the big toe. Damage to the toenail may result.

The best type of foot for *pointe* work has the first, second and possibly the third toes of relatively equal lengths. This permits a more even distribution of weight when standing *en pointe*.

Children with developing bunions should not work *en pointe*. Other forms and expectations of dance should be encouraged. Although anatomical factors may limit the amount and caliber of participation and perhaps the career possibilities a young person may have in ballet, they should not hamper the individual's desire to dance, according to one's own abilities, discipline, talent and pain-free enjoyment.

Biomechanical Factors

On a practical level biomechanics is concerned with the internal and external forces generated across a joint throughout the range of motion (ROM) of a joint, and their effect on other joints. For example, rolling inward (pronation) on the arch of the foot increases the stress on structures of the foot, and also inwardly twists the leg and strains the ligaments on the inner aspect of the knee joint.

Neither ballet nor the dancer understands or has any use for "normal" range of motion; minimal function is often minimal dancing—something which doesn't sell too many tickets. Ballet movements require full range of motion of the joints, especially of the lower extremity. The dancer's expectations are always at the extreme of any biomechanical or artistic consideration. In many instances, there is an almost inseparable interrelationship between anatomy, biomechanics and ballet technique and the development of injuries.

There are five critical biomechanical factors associated with development of dance-related injuries: (1) muscle imbalances of the hip, (2) tight calf muscles, (3) foot plantarflexion, (4) rigid first toe joint and (5) foot type.

Muscle Imbalances of the Hip

Normally, there are 45–50° of internal and external rotation. Professional dancers frequently develop tight, deep rotator muscles of the hip which limit their ability to turn-out.[2,3] This is not particularly surprising since these muscles are constantly and extensively used during all ballet movements. In addition, female dancers tend to have a greater amount of range of motion at the hip than male dancers, perhaps due to their earlier start in ballet. Apparently, turn-out is best developed prior to the ages of 10–14; a good genetic framework doesn't hurt either.

Limitation of hip rotation, especially external rotation, or turn-out can have a profound effect upon a dancer's technique and vulnerability to injury. A dancer may attempt to compensate for limited turn-out by tilting the pelvis, increasing the curvature of the lower spine, twisting the knees or abducting ("beveling") the front half of the foot (see exhibit 9-7). This is known among dancers as "forcing the turn-out." Dancers with inadequate turn-out may also use resin or slight moisture on the shoes to increase friction, place their feet in fifth position *demi-plié* and slowly straighten the legs. This "screwing the knee" is devastating to the medial aspect of the knee. A dancer with pain in this region should be suspected of forcing his or her turn-out. Compensating for poor turn-out may also increase the amount of stress placed upon the joints of the lower extremities, prevent proper alignment and increase pronation of the foot.

Although "perfect" turn-out theoretically involves 90° of external rotation at each hip, few dancers have as much as 70° of external rotation (see exhibit 9-8). Yet, many dancers can demonstrate adequate turn-out in the basic ballet positions. Turn-out involves a sufficient amount of external rotation at the hip (55–70°), external rotation at the knee (10°) and leg (12°) and abduction ("beveling") of the front half of the foot.

During a *grand plié*, the external rotation of the hip is superimposed upon the simultaneous actions of flexion and abduction of the thigh at the hip joint (see exhibit 9-8). The abduction of the thigh may allow for an additional amount of external rotation at the hip joint which is not accounted for during conventional testing of turn-out. In addition, dancers with tight hip muscles or joints will often compensate for decreased turn-out by tilting the pelvis forward and swaying the lower back. Functionally this increases the potential for turn-out, but, of course, ruins the body alignment and increases the chances of injury (see exhibit 9-7). The ability to naturally turn-out seems to be less of a factor than how you use it.

Although dancers are concerned only with turn-out, they would also agree that ballet requires efficient movement in all directions—a direct product of fluid, complete and balanced ROM of all the joints of the lower extremities. The hip series of exercises described in chapter 12 can be very effective in correcting these muscle imbalances as well as alleviating or diminishing some dancers' complaints of clicking noises or binding in the hip.

Tight Calf Muscles

The gastrocnemius and soleus muscles are powerful plantarflexors and invertors ("sickling") of the foot. These muscles insert onto the heel (calcaneus) by way of the Achilles tendon. When they are excessively tight, the foot cannot properly flex (dorsiflex) without making the foot much more rigid and non-shock absorbing. During the first 10° of the *demi-plié,* the foot must remain in a neutral position, that is not too rigid or too supple, for the foot to properly dissipate the forces of take-off and landing. Tight calf muscles limit the *demi-plié,* and seriously predisposes the dancer to overstress injuries of the foot and ankle. In some cases dorsiflexion of the ankle may be limited by bone spurs on the front of the ankle (anterior talar impingement syndrome) rather than tight calf muscles.

Professional dancers are very likely to develop tight calf muscles, more correctly called gastroc-soleus equinus. Equinus refers to the tendency of this condition to cause one to walk more on the balls of the feet—similar to horses. It is a common biomechanical problem among professional, advanced university and aerobic dancers as well as many competitive endurance athletes such as runners, and is related to the frequency, duration, intensity and technique of training.

Professional dancers acquire gastroc-soleus equinus as a result of years of extensive daily use of the calf muscles during the *demi-*

plié without a proportional amount of calf stretching. Technical faults such as the failure to allow the heels to contact the floor during the landing and take-off phases of the *demi-plié* may also contribute to this condition.

> A 16-year-old advanced female student in a major ballet school was referred to one of the authors by the director with a history of severe pain on the upper outer portion of her left leg. For the past six weeks she had been taking class every day and rehearsing *Les Patineurs* as an understudy.
>
> Biomechanical evaluation indicated a slight gastroc-soleus equinus, which was more prominent on the left. I observed her in class and noted that she repeatedly failed to allow the heels to contact the floor during the *plié*, especially in *petit allegro* combinations, and that she usually performed more movements on her left foot ("her turning leg"). I taught her a series of stretching exercises for her calves and feet (chapter 12), which she performed approximately six times a day. She was also told the importance of getting the heels down in the *demi-plié,* and to concentrate on this principle during all phases of the class. Three weeks later, she was completely asymptomatic, although *petit allegro* was still irritating and frustrating.

In an individual dancer, the presence of gastroc-soleus equinus, a technique that does not permit the heels to contact the ground, and a cavus (high-arched) foot-type, which is relatively non-shock absorbing but very fashionable these days, represents a serious predisposition to injuries of the foot, ankle and leg.

> While one of the authors was performing injury prevention evaluations for a company-affiliated ballet school, a young woman in her early twenties appeared at the door with a burly male escort and sweetly but firmly requested an immediate evaluation. Not knowing whether she was a dancer (she "looked" like a dancer), I explained the nature of the exam and proceeded with the evaluation. The biomechanical evaluation showed significant bilateral gastroc-soleus equinus, high-arched cavus feet and an unusual pattern of calluses on her feet that indicated either a very tight *pointe* shoe box or the practice of Chinese foot binding.

The results indicated that she was inordinately predisposed to Achilles tendinitis, medial ankle tenosynovitis and, most seriously, metatarsal stress fractures. With each word she and her friend became more upset until she finally burst in tears. At that time her friend informed me that she was the star principal dancer with a major ballet company and that she indeed had all of these problems, including three metatarsal stress fractures!

Later, we discussed at length effective methods of minimizing the chances of the recurrence of her injuries: wider boxes in her *pointe* shoes, calf stretching exercises, loading the heels during the *demi-plié* and better nutrition (she exhibited anorectic behavior, and almost certainly had caloric, protein, vitamin and mineral deficiencies).

Nevertheless, the conversation often returned to the premise that the company would take care of everything. She was their star; they wouldn't let anything happen to her. Her world was about fantasy—Odette/Odile and sylphs at midnight—not physical and financial reality. In the final analysis, she believed in denial and the company was a surrogate parent. By the age of 24 she was retired from dance due to chronic injuries—disenchanted with the betrayal of ballet.

Ankle Joint Plantarflexion

In professional ballet companies a dancer must be able to plantarflex (i.e., point or extend) the foot in such a way that the top of the foot falls in a direct line from the front edge of the shin (see exhibit 9-9). In the *demi-pointe* or *en pointe* positions this flexibility aligns the foot in a manner that allows the bones to bear the weight properly rather than the ligamentous and musculotendinous structures of the foot and ankle.

Although overarching of the foot is currently popular in many ballet companies, it can create biomechanical problems. Overarching *en pointe* greatly increases the amount of stress on the ligamentous and tendinous structures on the top of the foot (see exhibit 9-10). About 40 percent of professional female dancers have the range of motion necessary to overarch the foot. An appreciable number of these dancers complain about various strains on the dorsal aspect of the foot.[3]

If the foot cannot reach a high *demi-pointe*, the dancer's weight cannot be distributed over the balls of the feet (see exhibit 9-11). This serious misalignment increases the amount of stress placed upon the muscles, tendons and ligaments of the posterior, medial and lateral aspects of the ankle, thus increasing the vulnerability of these areas to injuries such as tendinitis, tenosynovitis (inflammation of the sheath around a tendon) and shin splints. The practice of beveling the foot while *en pointe* may allow a degree of shock absorption in the foot, but it may trigger the development of bunion deformities.

A limited ability to point the foot is an unsatisfactory and unemployable condition in aspiring dancers. In ballet there are fairly uncompromising aesthetic standards for beautifully pointed feet. A slightly flexed foot destroys the elongating illusion of the fully extended extremity. Female dancers must have a straight alignment of the pointed foot in order to perform *en pointe*, and men need it for *demi-pointe*. Functionally, dancers who are overweight and having difficulty rising to full *pointe* position demonstrate another type of limited plantarflexion. These conditions are not acceptable in most professional ballet companies in the United States.

Rigid First Toe Joint

In ballet the big toe (hallux) should be capable of dorsiflexing 90° in order for the foot to reach a high *demi-pointe* (see exhibit 9-12). Obviously this is more important in male dancers, who use the *demi-pointe* position more frequently, than it is in women, who work primarily *en pointe*. A fair number of professional dancers (30–40 percent) have less than 90° of dorsiflexion, and this type of stiff big toe joint (hallux rigidus) can lead to problems with technique. When rising to *demi-pointe*, the top edges of the big toe joint compress one another and frequently will inflame the joint capsule. Later on, bone spurs may develop in this area. If the joint becomes too stiff (<45°), you cannot *relevé* over the ball of your foot and your weight tends to pull you off of *demi-pointe*. No matter how much flexibility you have in your ankle joint, restricted dorsiflexion of the big toe will not permit a high *demi-pointe* (see exhibit 9-11). This is an excellent example of how limited range of motion in one joint compromises the function of another joint.

A dancer with hallux rigidus will roll towards the outside of the foot ("sickle the foot") during the *relevé* to *demi-pointe* or while performing movements on *demi-pointe*. Female dancers who have this condition may have difficulty rolling down through the foot from the *en pointe* position or rising to the *en pointe* position. If the stiffness becomes too severe, it may require surgery or a change to another form of dance that doesn't demand a high *demi-pointe*. Chapter 12 describes some exercises to minimize the development of hallux ridgidus by keeping the big toe joint flexible.

> A 26-year-old male principal dancer in a regional ballet company experienced needle-sharp pain in the back of the right ankle when he pointed his foot. During a dress rehearsal of *Giselle*, the abrupt pain from a *relevé* to *pirouette* caused his leg to reflexively relax, and he collapsed on stage. Examination of the right leg demonstrated a limited ability to point the right foot, which was painful when passively pointed to its limit (exhibit 9-11). In addition, he had limited dorsiflexion of the big toe (hallux rigidus) and chronically inflamed medial ankle tendons, especially the long tendon to the big toe (flexor hallucis longus). One year later, the right ankle required surgery to remove a bone spur on the back of the ankle along with the heavily calcified sheath of the flexor hallucis longus tendon. Although rehabilitation was successful, the dancer never returned to a full rehearsal/performance schedule. He is now pursuing a career in the fitness industry.

Foot Types

Another important factor about the ballet dancer's foot is the foot type: the flat foot and the high-arched foot. Currently, the high-arched foot (pes cavus) is the aesthetic favorite in ballet, although it is not by any means a requirement (see exhibit 9-6). Biomechanically, this foot type is relatively rigid and non-shock absorbing. In addition, the high-arched cavus foot may be associated with short Achilles tendon and tight calf muscles (gastroc-soleus equinus). The combination of the high-arched cavus foot, tight calf muscles and a dance technique that does not permit the heels to land in the *demi-plié* represents a serious potential injury situation for the dancer.

The flat foot presents both structural and functional problems to the dancer. In a flat foot (pes planus), the bones and ligaments of the foot are not structurally capable of supporting the arches of the foot. When standing on a flat foot, the inner arch of the foot collapses, causing the foot to roll inward or pronate. Although it is not as aesthetically pleasing to the eye as the high-arched foot, the flat foot is a very flexible, supple foot that absorbs a lot of shock—in fact, too much. Since the bone and ligaments are not supporting the foot, the long flexors of the toes and the plantarflexors of the foot have to work overtime to support the foot and absorb the shock of landing and push-off. Common injuries associated with flat feet include inflammation of the tendons of these muscles, shin splints on the inner aspect of the leg and plantar fasciitis at the base of the heel on the sole of the foot.

In athletes flat feet can be corrected by a mild arch support (orthotic). However, dancers usually do not have room in their shoes for orthotics. This ignores the fact that dance shoes are not sturdy enough to support orthotics, and the presence of arch supports in a ballet slipper destroys the line of the foot. Injuries related to flat feet can be minimized by avoiding an excessive amount of jumping and hopping movements—marking steps when possible and following a daily regimen of strengthening exercise for the feet (chapter 12).

Environmental Factors

Environmental factors that contribute to dance injuries may range from the ridiculous to the subtle: the famous case of the prima ballerina in *On Your Toes* being knocked off her toes and seriously injured by a wayward stage batten, or the dancer with a crippling sesamoiditis due to the placement of the seam on the sole of his ballet slipper. Sometimes it is a long cramped bus ride followed by a quick warm-up and performance in an unfavorable studio and theater. In fact climate control and dance floors in the studio or theater are common contributors to dance-related injuries.

Climate Control

Dancers frequently complain of cold or drafty studios and theaters. In some cases classes or performances may be outdoors in pavillion tents or amphitheaters; both cold and hot weather are obvious hazards. Cool temperatures make it difficult to warm-up properly or stay warmed-up. Dehydration, heat cramps, exhaustion or stroke are possible both outdoors and indoors.

> Prior to a performance of *Les Patineurs*, a graceful and amusing parody of the pleasures and perils of ice skating, the theater management waited until a half-hour before the audience arrived to turn on the air conditioner. Within ten minutes of the opening curtain, 200,000 watts of stage lighting and 2,000 warm bodies had shut down the air conditioner and created a 100° plus sauna on stage. Many of the sweating dancers, dressed in heavy waistcoats and long dresses, suffered from dehydration, heat cramps or exhaustion. On the lighter side, the finale was a sight to see. Amidst the gently falling snowflakes the spinning dancers looked like lawn sprinklers in a blizzard.

Floors

The resiliency and surface of the studio and stage floors can be critically important in the cause and prevention of injuries. The long- and short-term effects of performing on hard, non-compliant floors can be disastrously disabling even in the absence of other contributing factors. A number of injuries of the lower extremity, such as shin splints, inflammation of the tendons of the ankle and foot and stress fractures of the legs are attributable to dancing on hard floors. Dancers learn to adapt to hard floors by minimizing their exposure by "marking" (using gestures for certain movements) and increasing their *plié*.

> I learned the best lessons about the resiliency of dance floors when I first started dancing solos. The male variation in the "Bluebird Pas de Deux" requires 32 grueling *brisé volés* crossing diagonally from upstage left to downstage right. Initially, the concert hall floor was soft and compliant—almost buoyant—and I was flying. Midstage was the dancer's equivalent to "hitting the wall": The heavy steel stage traps sucked every ounce of energy from my thighs. Every step shook my bones. The final stretch of stage was soft—a marathon run in the sand. Only sheer willpower and fear made me finish. It

was not until after the performance that I realized I was injured. The next day the problem was diagnosed as a bone chip in the ankle joint. After that, I learned to watch out for those traps.

Hard, unforgiving floors or stages can be especially dangerous if they are located in important studios or theaters. The dancer may be compelled to dance on these hard surfaces because of the prestige of the studio or theater. A notorious example was the stage at Kennedy Center in Washington, D.C. Dancers complained for years about the hard stage and the resultant injuries. Finally, after the dancers' union threatened to boycott performances, a new floor was installed. Some union contracts now require a wood floor suspended over five shock absorbing layers of lattice-work. Progress, slow but sure.

Dancers have their preferences as to natural wood, linoleum or synthetic floor surfaces, depending upon the individual style of dance and previous experience. Most dance studios have wooden floors and permit the dancers to use rosin for friction. Many companies use an artificial vinyl surface for performances, yet frequently will not use them in the studio. Uniform traction, the absence of rosin or splinters, and in some cases a slight degree of additional resiliency make artificial dance floor surfaces highly desirable in the ballet studio and on the stage. With any surface it is imperative to keep it clean, smooth and free from irregularities or imperfections that may cause the dancer to slip or trip.

A few years ago, a famous ballerina told one of the authors a nightmarish story about her dance injury. After many years of self-imposed exile, George Balanchine had returned to his native country with his superb company, the New York City Ballet. On opening night at the Bolshoi Theatre, many eyes in the audience were looking for this extraordinarily talented young woman. Unfortunately, during her entrance, she slipped and fell on the slick floor and was knocked unconscious. The curtain had to be lowered in order to revive her. After a brief intermission, she was able to perform.

In retrospect, she commented that nothing could match the fear and horror she felt during that fall—the hopes and dreams of so many people dashed in an instant. Yet she recovered and so did everyone else. Both the company and she went on to astonishing success. To-

day she is widely considered one of the greatest ballerinas of all time.

Dietary and Nutritional Factors

The female ballet dancer is probably more of a reflection of a
particular society's perspective of women than we would casually
like to admit. Dancers epitomize in our own minds the self-
awareness, frustrations and distortions of our fat-conscious culture.
Practical medical guidelines and aesthetic criticisms of the ultralean "Balanchine" dancer have not changed the critical expectations
of the staff and public. As one principal dancer stated, "Ballet is a
visual art, and therefore we have a certain responsibility to look pre-
sentable to the paying public. Currently, there is absurd and danger-
ously unhealthy pressure from the public, staff and peers to be too
thin, despite the intelligence of knowing how bad it is."

Several nutrition-related situations may contribute to an injury: (1) overweight, (2) underweight, (3) fatigue and anemia and
(4) muscle spasms due to mineral imbalances.

Overweight

Generally, overweight is a more significant factor among university and private studio dancers than among professional dancers.
"To be a dancer is to be thin," and an overweight dancer is virtually
unemployable in a professional ballet company in the United States.
In spite of this opinion, many professional dancers believe that it is
healthier to be slightly overweight or average weight than to be underweight. Still, the majority know that they must be lean to be
seen. In addition, a dancer who is overweight may have problems in
controlling technique, such as rising *en pointe*.

> A 19-year-old, slightly overweight semi-professional fe-
> male dancer in a civic ballet company came to one of the
> authors during a rehearsal of *The Nutcracker*. During
> the brisk hopping movements *(ballonne)* of the marzi-
> pan dance, she developed a sharp pain in the right big
> toe. Examination of her toe indicated chronic damage to
> the inner edge of the toenail, thickening of the nail and
> fresh blood under the nail. The bone at the tip of the big
> toe was also very tender. The digit was packed in ice and

the dancer was taken to the emergency room. Radiographs indicated a fracture of the big toe.

Later examination of her nearly-new *pointe* shoes showed the collapse (more accurately, crushing) of the inner edge of the shoe box. Older pairs were even worse. Clearly, she had not been standing squarely *en pointe*. The director commented that her *pointe* problems had progressively worsened as she gained weight. During her recovery and rehabilitation, the dancer was started on a balanced dietary program (chapter 8), lost eight pounds (to 17 percent body fat) and worked on proper body alignment in class. Her stance *en pointe* greatly improved, and *relevé en pointe* was also easier with less weight—much to the relief of her big toe.

Underweight

America's obsession with leanness is epidemic in dance and is further compounded by the enormous occupational bias in favor of thin dancers. Although most dancers think that being underweight is healthiest, this is not always a safe or reasonable assumption. Over the past 12 years, one of the authors' experience with dancers at all levels of participation, from small studios, universities and company-affiliated schools to civic, regional, national and international ballet companies, clearly places the problem of excessively lean dancers at the top of each hierarchy. In general, the impetus for the occurrence of excessively underweight dancers are directly proportional to the competitiveness and professional status of the school or company. Elite dancers in highly competitive national or international ballet schools or companies are much more likely to be excessively lean than are members of local studios or non-professional troupes. In fact, amateur dancers more typically reflect the trends in the general population for their age group, and quite often overweight is a more significant problem.

Many dancers who are excessively lean are often protein and carbohydrate deficient. This, of course, makes it difficult for the body to build, maintain and repair tissue—essential events for optimal physical performance and rehabilitation. Despite the fact that none of the Ballet West dancers were overweight, half thought that they had a weight problem, and 70 percent of the dancers were dieting. However, measurements of body fat indicated that the female dancers had about 16 percent and the male dancers about 12 percent body fat—optimal percentages for just about any male or female athlete, and virtually the same as measurements on dancers from the American Ballet Theatre, New York City Ballet, San Francisco Ballet and Cleveland Ballet. Despite these optimal values of body fat, the dancers were still inordinately concerned with dieting, and considered themselves overweight from the perspective of the dance company or school.

There is a possibility that ultra-leanness, along with the associated nutritional deficiencies and physical demands of dance, may contribute to delayed menarche (the onset of periods or menses) and the development of menstrual irregularities. Delayed menarche and menstrual abnormalities have been reported in dancers from Ballet West (38 percent), American Ballet Theatre (47 percent) and the Cleveland Ballet (50 percent). Most interesting, there is evidence that highly athletic women with absent or irregular menses (periods) have an almost threefold increased risk of stress fractures, perhaps due to the negative effects of a reduction of estrogen hormone (E_2) and its effect on bone density. Dietary calcium deficiency may further compound this situation.

Fatigue and Anemia

In dance, fatigue is most commonly due to the long hours of practice and performance, but it may also be attributable to caloric- and iron-deficient diets. Dancers generally do not eat enough food to supply optimal levels of energy and nutrients for work and repair of tissues. Dancers from Ballet West and the Ballet West Summer Program reported an average daily caloric intake of only 1420 and 1760 calories, respectively. This caloric deficiency corresponds with studies of the Cleveland Ballet (1358 calories/day) and American Ballet Theatre (1673 calories/day). All corroborate the fact that female professional dancers consume an inadequate amount of calories and are also protein, carbohydrate and iron deficient. Iron deficiencies are more pronounced in women with regular menstrual cycles, and manifest themselves as severe, lingering fatigue. A balanced diet (see chapter 8) and perhaps an iron supplement can correct all of these problems and still keep the dancer at a lean, optimal dancing weight.

Muscle Spasms

Muscle spasms may be due to localized microscopic tears in the muscles, lactic acid accumulation in the muscle or electrolyte imbalances. Most muscle spasms respond well to gentle massage and stretching and heat applications. Spasms due to a mineral imbalance may be due to overexertion in a warm environment, inadequate nutrition or eating disorders such as bulimia. Although many dancers take multivitamin and mineral supplements, calcium or potassium deficiencies or imbalances have been documented. Heavy physical exercising may result in a temporary reduction of sodium and potassium and may be a factor in triggering muscle spasms, along with an inadequate dietary intake of calcium or self-abusive eating behavior such as vomiting or the use of laxatives or diuretics.

Psychological Factors

Dance is a tough profession—both physically and mentally. We have discussed numerous factors which contribute to physical injury; however, dancers suffer more than their fair share of mental stresses and strains: depression, unemployment, competition, burn out, not to mention the mental anxiety, frustration and despair that go along with any job-threatening injury or disability.

Dancers take these physical and mental risks, oftentimes knowingly and willingly, just for the opportunity to dance, not just to be in the spotlight or for the glory and recognition. There's not enough of that to ever compensate for the singular dedication of a young life to dance.

What is it that makes dancers want to dance? To ignore the sacrifices and risks demanded of a performing artist? The psychological reasons for the pursuit of perfect expression intrinsic to performing are understandable. The joy of dancing for someone else—family or friends—has long since passed. Perhaps dancers like the recognition, the accolades and adulation of faceless, nameless strangers in a theater. It may be more fundamental than that.

The rituals of ancient cultures were dances of feast and famine, mating and marriage, life and death, Gods and demigods, light and dark, good and bad—primal acts about the nature of our survival, perseverance and perpetuation. Dance is spun out of the limbic core of our cerebrum and strewn onto the private stage of our lives.

Dancers are not athletes; to equate the two is to do both an injustice. They are similar in their movements, but differ in their purpose; like comparing the brush strokes of Rembrandt to those of a house painter. Dance is a mental game played on a physical field of battle. It is in this mental game that the determination, concentration, competition and peer pressure take their toll of casualties. These factors filter out more than half of the up-and-coming young talent. Mental demands and risks—like the physical ones—are a part of the reality of dance.

The mental stresses of fierce competition and glaring peer pressure were discussed in chapter 1, "The Dancer's World." In addition to these, there are other psychological factors that either cause or contribute to an injury or represent an injury in their own right.

Anorectic Behavior/Bulimia

Currently, anorexia nervosa is a sensitive and sensationalized subject in America. Clinical anorexia nervosa, however, is probably as rare among professional dancers as it is among the general population. It is very difficult to have severe anorexia and maintain the energy levels necessary to dance six to ten hours a day. Nevertheless, there are dancers who exhibit some anorectic characteristics, such as the distortion of body image, preoccupation with excessive leanness and self-abusive behavior such as semi-starvation, self-induced vomiting and laxative abuse.

Most anorectic behavior is found in the highly competitive professional ballet schools and companies. In this situation, anorectic behavior can have disastrous physical, psychological and financial consequences to the affected dancer. Much of its prevalence may be attributed to cutthroat competition, highly critical peer and public pressure and punitive, capricious aesthetic standards. In *most* dance companies and studios, however, the incidence of anorectic behavior is probably not significantly different from the general population or other female athletes when adjusted for age, level of activity and social status. This is not to say that there aren't already far too many dancers, athletes and individuals who exhibit anorectic behavior. On the contrary, it is much too common of a disorder. Anorexia can, of course, be life threatening, and the extremely poor nutrition and muscle-wasting of anorectic behavior can seriously affect physical performance, growth and repair.

Bulimia or self-induced vomiting as a means of weight control has reached epidemic proportions in our society. It is extremely common among middle to upper class, high school and college age women. In some dormitories, the acrid stench of vomitus is quite noticeable in many of the bathrooms. Self-induced vomiting as a dietary manipulation goes back a long way.

In ancient Roman times, senators would gorge themselves at a huge feast (similar to the modern day salad bar) and then excuse themselves to the vomitorium, where they would throw up. Within minutes, they were back at the table for seconds (vomiting indirectly stimulates the appetite centers in the brain). I've often wondered if the chef was flattered or insulted by this nonstop binge/purge competition. This may very well have been the first fad diet, the Roman Diet Plan: "All you can eat at the tip of your finger."

The practice of bulimia may prevent sizable gains in body weight, but it is not an effective method of long-term weight loss and carries with it considerable physical ramifications. Chronic self-induced vomiting corrodes tooth enamel, enlarges the salivary glands on the sides of the face, leatherizes the epithelial lining of the throat and disrupts the potassium and pH balance in the body. Most perceptive clinicians can recognize a chronic bulimic after a physical exam and urine analysis. Bulimia, however, is more than a physical problem; it is a psychological disturbance with physical manifestations.

Anorexia and bulimia are serious eating disorders that require medical and psychological treatment. Fortunately, there has been a recent proliferation of clinics and psychological support groups designed specifically for individuals with eating disorders. Aside from offering treatment, these groups help the individual understand the cause of their problem, place it in the proper psycho-socio-cultural perspective and prevent its recurrence.

In their relentless pursuit for thinness dancers lose their bearings on what is considered a normal body image. Dancers view their bodies in the mirror like the rest of us see ourselves in a fun house mirror—distorted and disproportionate. They, however, don't find it particularly amusing. There is a critical need to define clearly the elements of the spectrum from healthy leanness to anorectic behavior to clinical anorexia. Medical science hasn't done enough to define this spectrum. Although many dancers are extremely lean, they are not necessarily unhealthy or anorectic. Dancers need to know that it is possible to be lean and healthy by following sound nutritional principles (chapter 8).

Psychological Burnout

Many professional dancers grew up under the dominant influence of a ballet studio, school or academy. For those dancers who live at a professional ballet school, the school becomes a surrogate parent to the young dancers, nurturing their growth into professional dancers. Most of their waking lives are concerned with becoming dancers. Eventually, some individuals become psychologically fatigued and they can take no more; they are "burned out." The associated physical fatigue, mental malaise and inattentiveness can expose the dancer to unnecessary errors of technique, training or judgment.

Other Psychological Factors

Dancers don't always stop dancing because of physical injuries. With age, dance technique may slowly slip away and with it the allegiance of an adoring, appreciative public. Dancers believe that the body is the imperfect instrument in the perfect art. When the disparity becomes too great between the two, it's time to flee to other careers that are more respected, stable or secure (see chapter 13).

Performing is full of contrasts and contradictions—the elation of entertaining and the strain of training every day. At one moment dancers have the attention and adoration of the masses, at another, anonymity and depersonalized criticism. Post-performance depression is a part of the dancer's reality. In one survey of dancers in New York City, more than 70 percent of the professional dancers experienced depression, 12 percent used tranquilizers and 30 percent were seeking psychological counseling.[1] A recent well-publicized suicide of a principal dancer with the New York City Ballet was a tragic reminder of these pressures.

For some young discerning dancers the austere life of the suffering artist is not a very attractive profession and their talents are best expressed elsewhere. Some dancers may stop dancing because of a sense of betrayal by the company—a feeling that the same company that nurtured them as developing artists failed to care for them as adults (see the case history on pp. 111-12). The benevolence of the professional ballet school is replaced by the harsh realism of the company. Talented young dancers, who are trained as artists, become a commodity in a very difficult business.

Conclusion

Dance places enormous physical and psychological demands upon the human body and brain. After many years of training and a few years of performing, all dancers must eventually start new careers. If a physician was told that after seven years of training he would be able to practice for only a few years, would he still want to become a physician? Dancers are clearly dedicated to the dance.

Ballet is also big business. Ballet companies in the United States are multimillion dollar corporations in which the dancer is frequently viewed as an expendable commodity. A large ballet company may spend $200,000 or more per year caring for and replacing disabled dancers. Many of these tragic injuries could have been prevented if a fraction of that money was spent on analyzing the causes of dance-related injuries and developing effective injury prevention programs. American companies need to wake up to the critical importance of protecting the medical and occupational needs of this precious artistic resource.

Exhibit 9-1.
Causes of Dance-related Injuries

Exhibit 9-2.
The Cycle of Injury

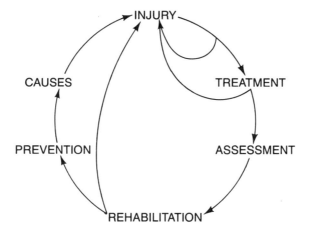

Exhibit 9-3.
Training History of Ballet Dancers*

Dancers	Starting Age	Total Years of Training	Years at This Level
Female professionals N = 24	8.6 ± 2.1	12.7 ± 3.6	5.1 ± 2.2
Male professionals N = 15	12.3 ± 4.2	13.0 ± 4.8	7.2 ± 3.4
Female students N = 77	7.3 ± 3.4	8.2 ± 2.8	2.7 ± 1.2
Male students N = 11	16.3 ± 2.1	4.0 ± 2.7	0.7 ± 1.1

*In years

Exhibit 9-4.
Training Workload of Ballet Dancers*

Dancers	Class	Rehearsal	Performance	Total
Female professionals N = 24	10.2 ± 2.3	26.6 ± 6.1	7.9 ± 3.6	44.7 ± 4.0
Male professionals N = 15	9.3 ± 0.9	26.1 ± 6.2	9.5 ± 5.3	44.9 ± 4.1
Female students N = 77	13.6 ± 6.1	**	**	**
Male students N = 11	17.3 ± 7.7	**	**	**

*In average hours of participation per week
**Rehearsal and performance work loads for advanced students were not included.

Exhibit 9-5.

The "Balanchine body" in first arabesque.

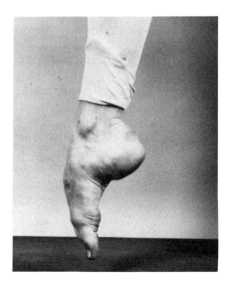

Exhibit 9-6.

Plantarflexed cavus foot. At least 90° of plantarflexion is required when pointing the foot. This ideal example demonstrates a perfectly pointed, high-arched foot, an aesthetic standard in ballet.

Exhibit 9-7.

Poor turn-out in second position. In order to compensate for poor turn-out, dancers frequently tilt the pelvis to increase the external ROM of the hip. The resultant hyperlordosis and poor body alignment are not only amusing, but also quite dangerous.

Exhibit 9-8.

Perfect *plié* in second position. Dancers dream of having turn-out and a *plié* like this. Notice the perfect alignment of feet, knees, and body. A few years later, this 14-year-old became an international prize winner and a leading dancer with a major ballet company.

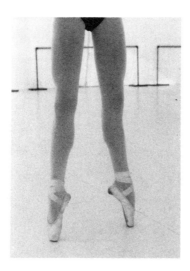

Exhibit 9-9.

Normal feet *sur les pointes.* The line of gravity for each foot should extend through the tibia and bones of the foot to the tips of the toes.

Exhibit 9-10.

Overarching of the foot on *pointe* is currently fashionable in ballet. However, overarching may stress the ligaments on the dorsum of the foot as well as damage the toenails, because the line of gravity falls on a point anterior to the dorsum of the foot rather than through the foot.

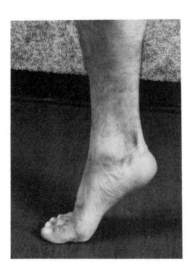

Exhibit 9-11.

Abnormal *demi-pointe.* This dancer demonstrates limited
plantarflexion due to posterior impingement and hallux rigidus. In
dancers, ankle joint plantarflexion and first metatarsophalangeal
dorsiflexion must be analyzed separately.

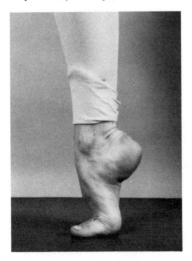

Exhibit 9-12.

Normal *demi-pointe.* An excellent example of the amount of ROM
in the ankle joint and first metatarsophalangeal joint in the
demi-pointe position. The weight is distributed directly to the heads
of the metatarsals. Male dancers use the *demi-pointe* position
extensively, especially during pirouettes.

References

1. PACH Survey. Dance Medicine Health Newsletter 1983; 2(1):3.
2. Stephens RE. Biomechanical aspects of ballet and ballet injuries (Slide cassette). Minneapolis, MN; McGraw-Hill, 1982.
3. Stephens RE. The biomechanical aspects of injuries in elite ballet dancers. *La Recherche en Danse.* Universite de Paris-Sorbonne, 1986.
4. Stephens RE. The etiology of injuries in professional ballet dancers. *La Recherche en Danse.* Universite de Paris-Sorbonne, 1986.
5. Ryan AJ and RE Stephens. *Dance Medicine: A Comprehensive Guide.* Pluribus Press and The Physician and Sportsmedicine: Chicago, 1987.

10

DANCE INJURIES

Few people have any idea about the dangers or types of injury possible in the different forms of dance, although most have a general idea about the dangers of injury in sports in general, and sometimes quite a bit of knowledge about injuries in one sport or another. This is in part due to the fact that the daily newspapers have sports pages where they can read every day about sports injuries, but when the paper reports about dance—which is not often—it usually is only a critique of a performance. Injury is seldom mentioned. Many people have had some personal experience in one or another form of dance and seldom, if ever, had an injury as a result. There's a lot known about the personal lives of prominent athletes from reading sports magazines but little about the personal lives of dancers except for the very few at the top of the pyramid.

Studies in the field that we now call Dance Medicine stand in a position similar to that in which Sports Medicine stood 40 years ago. There is no system for collecting information about the occurrence of dance injuries, although there is some experience regarding claims for Workmen's Compensation from professional dancers in New York State in recent years. There is no professional organization including physicians, therapists, choreographers and others who assist and supervise dancers to stimulate education, research and service in the field of dance in contrast to the many in physical education and sport. The National Dance Association of the American Alliance for Health, Physical Education, Recreation and Dance is concerned principally with teaching and performance.

Publications from individuals, groups and institutions working with dancers that relate to the occurrence of injuries in dance, their causes, prevention and treatment have been relatively few and report experiences limited by the particular interests and personal experiences of those who are writing them. The first comprehensive text in English, *Dance Medicine: A Comprehensive Guide*, which collected the available information in reports from physicians and other professionals working with dancers around the world, was published in 1987.

Related Factors

What we do know about injuries in dancers comes chiefly from reports of their occurrences in professional dance companies in ballet and the students in their schools. A study of professional dancers from Ballet West and advanced students from their Summer Program in 1982–1983 showed that 90 percent of the professional dancers and 63 percent of the students had suffered a dance related injury at some time in their careers. The professionals had almost twice as many injuries as the students and three-fifths had some temporary or permanent disability as a result, compared to one-half of the students. The female students had the lowest injury rate (61 percent) among the four groups and the frequency for the male students was the same as for the male professionals.

We know also from long observation of and experience in working with dancers that the majority of injuries from which they suffer are due to overuse rather than from falls, collisions, sudden twists or strains. Many injuries in ballet appear to be associated with poor technique, as A.J.G. Howse, physician to the Royal Ballet, has observed. It is the repeated exposure rather than one incident that causes the damage. The heavy schedules of class, rehearsal and performance each day for six or seven days each week the year around are chiefly responsible. In the soft tissues the effects of overuse are expressed in acute and chronic inflammation of muscles, tendons, ligaments and bursas. In the skeleton they are expressed as stress fractures. Because the correction for overuse is rest, at least in a modified form that puts the injured part at rest, and because the professional dancer has little chance to do this, the acute injury becomes chronic and may lead to more serious and disabling developments of rupture or fibrosis.

Because different parts of the body may suffer the same types of injury, and since the treatment of the particular type is very similar no matter what part of the body is affected, further discussion of dance injuries here will be divided by body part rather than type. This will also show why some parts are more commonly injured in dancers and how this knowledge may help in treatment and rehabilitation following injury.

Injuries by Body Part

In five reports of injuries in ballet dancers, two in theatrical dancers, two in dance students and one in modern dancers, the greatest number of injuries were found in the lower extremities from the knee down. Injuries to the knee and ankle were about equal in numbers, followed by the foot and leg in that order. Injuries to the lower back and hip appeared more common in the modern and theatrical dancers. Relatively few injuries to the neck and upper extremities were reported. Between the different styles practiced in ballet and modern dance there was some variation in the numbers of injuries reported, but it did not appear significant.

Foot and Ankle

When the skin of the sole of the foot is dry and callused it may split, rip or tear. This is most likely to happen to those who dance in bare feet, typically modern dancers. Small deposits of rosin or pieces of discarded chewing gum may catch and hold the skin as the dancers turns on the ball or heel of the foot. Splits in callused skin do not heal, and a fissure in the normal skin beneath may form unless the callused skin is shaved off below the depth of the split. Regular use of an oil or cream on the sole may prevent such splitting. When a fissure occurs it may heal if covered with a patch of white adhesive tape that protects it from further pulling, holds it together and helps keep it clean.

Blisters occur on the sole, around the heel and on the toes partly as an overuse injury but also because of poorly fitting hose or shoes. They can be temporarily disabling as well as painful and may become infected if not managed properly. A thin coating of petroleum jelly (Vaseline) may help in prevention. Once a blister has formed you must try to preserve the roof, if possible, to protect the sensitive skin beneath it. The fluid can be aspirated through a needle inserted through intact skin near the blister. Adhesive tape over the roof of a small blister will allow it to reattach itself in a few days. With a large blister the roof may be cut through half way around to evacuate the fluid. A light spray of clear tape adhesive on the floor of the blister will allow the roof to reattach. If a blister is infected the roof should be removed and an antibiotic ointment applied under a dressing.

Hemorrhage under a toenail may result from stubbing a toe, the toe being pushed down too hard into a very tight toe box or someone stepping on the toe. The pain may be relieved by drilling through the nail to release the blood. If this is done very soon after the injury the nail may adhere to its bed and not be lost.

Deep, sometimes called "stone" bruises of the foot may involve the soft tissues such as muscles, tendons, ligaments, fat pads and bursas, but may also affect the coverings of the foot bones, the periosteum. These are usually felt beneath the heel or in and around the heads of the metatarsal bones. They arise chiefly from hard landings on unyielding surfaces, often with shoes that offer little or no cushioning against the impact. In considering such an injury as a cause of pain across the metatarsal heads in the ball of the foot, make sure that the cause is not the degenerative change in the head of a metatarsal called Freiberg's infraction (see page 139) or the small tumor that may involve a nerve running between the metatarsal heads called Morton's neuroma (see page 139). Both are more serious and the latter may require surgical removal. Pain in the heel (calcaneodynia) may be due to inflammation in the fat pad that cushions the heel, an inflamed bursa on, beneath or behind the heel bone, or an inflamed intrinsic muscle such as the abductor of the great toe or a stress fracture of the calcaneus. These bruises will heal in time but since the dancers continue to put pressure on them they must be padded or cushioned in some way to relieve this pressure.

The toes of the dancer may become deformed because of the pressures to which they are subjected from bearing the dancer's weight, from the constantly repeated flexion and extension in the interphalangeal and at the metatarsophalangeal joints, and from the types of shoes worn. The tendons which attach to them may become inflamed from overuse and may shorten or rupture; the ligaments of the joints become stretched or torn causing instability; the cartilages in the joint spaces are damaged; the bones may dislocate or be involved in stress or displaced fractures.

Corns (hyperkeratoses) can occur over any bony prominence on the forefoot and between the toes, where they are usually called "soft" corns but are particularly painful. They are common on top of the second and fifth proximal joints between the toe phalanges but may occur over any of the joints between the metatarsals and phalanges and at the tips of the toes. Corns may occur between the toes where the second, third and fourth toes are of approximately equal length instead of forming a rainbow arc.

Since corns are caused by pressure one of the most important things to do in their treatment is to attempt to relieve the pressure. Because women are traditionally and typically sensitive about shoe sizes, it may be difficult to persuade a ballerina that she needs a larger *pointe* shoe. Other measures, however, such as stuffing cotton between and around the toes and using dispersive felt padding, may be only temporarily successful in relieving the pain. It may not be possible to relieve the pressure entirely, and looked at in this light the corn serves as protection. Indiscriminate surgical removal, if it exposes underlying sensitive points, may do more harm than good. Paring down the corn periodically with fine sandpaper or a scalpel, together with other means of relieving pressure, may be the best solution.

Three cautions should be observed in approaching corns directly. The first is that unless you are very experienced in paring them it is better to leave this to a podiatrist or a surgeon. The second is that the corn may be secondarily infected, which may require treatment with an antibiotic to cure the infection and keep it from spreading. The third is that if it is not already infected, your self-treatment may cause an infection if not done carefully and antiseptically. Repeated use of keratolytic plasters may do more harm than good.

Warts (verrucae) are not caused by injury but by a virus. This virus is contagious, and when the papillomas they create are fresh and active the virus can be spread by close physical contact, by using the same towel as someone who has it or by wearing their shoes. They seem relatively common on dancers' feet and can be painful to pressure on the soles of the feet. There is no truly effective treatment to eliminate them. If cut out they tend to recur at the same site. You might have some success using a preparation of salicylic acid in a collodion base (Salactic liquifilm) combined with abrasion with a pumice stone. Whatever you do try not to get through the full thickness of the skin, which may give you a sensitive scar. If you are very patient they may disappear spontaneously, but it may take three to five years, a long time in the relatively short career of a dancer.

If you are having pain in the anterior transverse metatarsal arch, which is made up by the heads of the metatarsals, your podiatrist or physician may suggest an x-ray and after viewing it say that you are suffering from Freiberg's infraction. That may sound terrible, but it explains why you have had redness, tenderness and swelling both on the tops and soles of your feet near the center of that arch, and why the foot is painful even at rest sometimes. What has happened is that the growing portion of one of the metatarsal heads (usually the second) is suffering from a poor blood supply and is degenerating. The x-ray shows it to appear flattened. The use of dispersive padding to relieve pressure on the head and modified rest will help it to heal, but it takes months. Continuing to dance without some relief may result in the growth plate of the bone slipping off and the bone putting out spurs, either or both of which might end your dancing career.

Another cause of pain in this metatarsal arch is a small tumor of the sensory nerve passing down between the metatarsal heads to the toes. It is named after the physician who was the first to describe it, Thomas G. Morton, and so is called Morton's neuroma. It should not be confused with Morton's neuralgia or Morton's foot, both named after the same man. This neuroma appears to be due to pressure on the nerve from the squeezing together of the metatarsal heads, especially the third and fourth. Adding a half size to the length or width of the ballet shoe may correct this. Some adult ballerinas still wear the same size shoe as when they were students. A felt pad placed in the center of the sole just behind the anterior metatarsal arch in the ballet and street shoes may also relieve it by allowing the arch to spread itself. Since the ballerina is seldom flat on her feet this may help only in the street shoe. When none of these things help you must seek the help of the podiatrist or surgeon to have the little tumor removed. This will give complete relief and you should be able to dance again in a few weeks.

Morton's foot occurs when the second toe is long and the great toe short. This tends to shift the weight, which is normally borne 50 percent on the head of the first metatarsal with the other 50 percent distributed over the other four. There is also an increased space between the first and second metatarsal. The resulting pressure causes a large callus beneath the second metatarsal head and may cause pain on walking or running. Relief is obtained by putting a felt pad under the first metatarsal head to shift the weight back to it and away from the second.

Morton's neuralgia is pain in the fourth metatarsal head and is due to the capsule and ligaments holding this bone to the first (proximal) phalanx of the fourth toe being severely stretched or torn, allowing the head to slip upward toward the top of the foot and dragging or compressing the nerve between the two metatarsals. This is an overuse injury and most often seen in older dancers. The only solution is to remove the metatarsal head and tighten and suture the supporting ligaments of the metatarsophalangeal joint.

Fractures of the toes other than the great toe are seldom greatly displaced and are usually treated by strapping the injured toe to the adjacent toe with some cotton padding between the toes. Any fracture of the great toe is serious because it is the toe from which the dancer pushes off in any position except when on *pointe*. Fracture of the end (distal) phalanx may be reduced by an orthopedic surgeon, who will correct any displacement by inserting a surgical (Kirschner) wire to realign the position of the fragments. Healing takes a matter of weeks rather than days. Fractures of the proximal phalanx are usually displaced and will require surgical reduction, often with wiring, application of a cast and no weight bearing for six to eight weeks. Sometimes such a fracture will be associated with a rupture of the ligaments supporting the metatarsophalangeal joint. This requires surgical repair or the toe will never be stable. Dislocation of the small toes can usually be easily reduced and held in place by taping until the ligaments are healed.

Every fracture is technically a stress fracture but the ones called such typically have a crack or split in the bone but no separation of the fragments. They result typically not from one sudden stress, blow or twist, but as a result of repeated strain-producing small cracks in the structure of the bone until the effect becomes great enough to produce the pain and local tenderness that indicate something has happened. A plain x-ray at first may not show the cracks or any loss of bone substance, but now this can be demonstrated by a special x-ray with the injection into a vein of a radioactive substance which localizes at the site of the problem and shows up as a "hot spot," or by the use of ultrasound imaging, which displays a three-dimensional image of the bone.

Such fractures are serious for dancers because they are painfully disabling and if neglected or untreated can produce a displaced fracture, which then needs to be set and perhaps immobilized in a cast. Stress fractures are relatively common because of the overuse to which the skeleton is subject in dance. The metatarsal bones are the most common site but they can occur in the tarsal bones, particularly the talus, cuneiform and calcaneus and in the ankle. To think that these fractures will heal without reducing the stress that caused them (in this case a heavy schedule of class, rehearsal and performance) and by simply using some padding and strapping is an indulgence in wishful thinking. Even when you relieve the stress by reducing the schedule and cutting down weight bearing it takes weeks, even months, for healing to occur. The question you have to face as a dancer is whether you are willing to give up the necessary time when the diagnosis is made to return to normal activity or to limp along partially disabled for weeks and months and risk a result that may end your dance career entirely. You need the best qualified advice you can get on this situation from a podiatrist or orthopedist.

A bursa is a sac lined with a synovial membrane, which is the same as the lining of a joint. It lies between a tendon and a bone, a tendon and a ligament or between other structures where friction may occur and reduces friction by allowing smooth gliding motions. The membrane secretes a fluid, synovia, which helps make this possible. As a result of repeated impacts or overuse the bursa may become inflamed and painful, increasing its secretion of fluid until it can be felt as a distended sac or even seen prominently beneath the skin. In some locations where a bursa is not normally present, as between a tendon near its insertion into a bone and the skin, a bursa called an adventitial bursa may form. There are two natural bursas and one adventitial bursa in the foot that may be inflamed in dancers. The first lies beneath the Achilles tendon near its insertion into the calcaneus and over the posterior tubercle of the calcaneus. The second lies under the inferior tubercle of the calcaneus and over the fat pad of the heel. The adventitial bursa may appear beneath the skin over the lower portion of the Achilles tendon.

When a bursa is inflamed it becomes painful and the pain is aggravated by any motion over or around it. It is tender to touch and if it is close to the skin there will be redness of the overlying skin. Over time the constant pain may disappear but will recur on motion and fluid secretion may increase. In this chronic stage there may be small deposits of calcium in and around the bursa which give a sensation of crackling or may produce an audible click on motion. Treatment for the acute inflammation is local application of ice and giving non-steroidal anti-inflammatory medication such as ibuprofen (Advil) by mouth. If pain is severe and persistent your physician may inject the bursa with a mixture of a local anesthetic and a corticosteroid. Where considerable fluid is present this may be aspirated before the medication is injected. Where bursitis is chronic and resistant to medication, especially when there is considerable calcification, the bursa may have to be removed surgically.

Tendinitis is acute inflammation of a tendon and its covering or sheath that results typically from overuse. The tendons around the foot and ankle commonly involved are the Achilles, flexor of the great toe, posterior tibial and peroneal. All these tendons in the ballet dancer are put under severe and repeated strain by the forcible plantar flexion involved in dancing on *pointe* and *demi-pointe*. Those that pass under the foot are also affected by the forcible planting of the foot, slapping the foot and landing on it from jumps. This is a very disabling condition requiring rest with medication in the acute stages. In chronic resistant cases surgery may be necessary.

Achilles tendinitis is the most common of these conditions and also the most resistant to treatment because it is almost impossible for the dancer to stop dancing long enough for it to heal. When dancing resumes there is a strong tendency for it to recur. The mainstay of treatment is the non-steroidal anti-inflammatory medication. Injection of corticosteroid medication around the tendon or into its sheath is dangerous since it may aggravate the tendency of the tendon to degenerate and perhaps rupture. In chronic cases a surgical stripping of the sheath and repair of the tendon may be necessary, but this produces a prolonged disability. If the tendon ruptures it should be repaired and reinforced with a graft from other local available tissue.

The second most common, and potentially most serious, site of tendinitis in the dancer is in the large flexor of the great toe. It may produce the condition known as functional hallux limitus, or in the end stage hallux rigidus, which means respectively that the tendon won't move the way that it should or that it won't move at all. Pain is produced when the foot is dorsiflexed, which causes passive dorsiflexion of the hallux. The activities which bring this about and create overuse in ballet are *relevé, demi-* and *grand plié*. The trouble starts where the tendon lies in a groove on the posterior tubercle of the talus. When the foot is extended, as in these positions, the tendon is stretched between the tubercle and sustentaculum of the talus. As the process continues inflammation progresses to degeneration and the tendon may rupture. Relief may be offered by anti-inflammatory medication, local ice massage and using a metatarsal pad with a sesamoid extension in shoes worn for activities other than dancing. The dancer may tape a similar felt pad to the foot for class and rehearsal. In the long run surgical correction for this tendon and the posterior tibial tendon, which is adjacent and often also involved, may be necessary. For severe hallux rigidus it is always necessary.

Sesamoid bones (so-called because they usually resemble the oval shape of the sesame seed) lie in tendons which move across bony surfaces. The kneecap patella is the most familiar example. In the dancer's foot there are three that may be injured and fractured or cause secondary inflammation in the tendon: the medial and lateral sesamoids in the split tendon of the short flexor of the hallux and one over the navicular bone on its lateral surface. The so-called os trigonum that lies just behind the talus is not a sesamoid but simply an old fragment of the posterior tubercle of the talus which has become a separate entity.

Fractures of the sesamoids may be difficult to find on x-ray examination unless a bone scan is used. The sesamoids beneath the hallux may become trapped beneath the adjacent metatarsal head if the hallux is very long. These injuries may be treated by placing a rocker mechanism in the street shoes which can be fitted by a shoemaker and using a sesamoid pad or other dispersive padding. You should consult your podiatrist or physician to do this because you need expert advice and assistance to get it right. If all else fails it is possible to have one or both sesamoids removed surgically without appreciably impairing your ability to dance.

The most common injury to the ankle in dancers is the sprain. Sprains of the ligaments or the outer side of the ankle outnumber those to the inner side by about four to one. A principal reason for this is that the ligaments on the inner side form a broad band, giving them the name of deltoid because that is their shape. There are five ligaments on the outer side, well separated from each other and none very strong individually. These ligaments from the front to the back are the anterior inferior tibio-fibular, the anterior talo-fibular, the calcaneofibular, the posterior talo-fibular and the posterior tibio-fibular. The one most commonly injured is the anterior inferior tibio-fibular. The one critical to the stability of the ankle is the anterior talo-fibular. Often two or more will be sprained at the same time.

A sprain of the ankle is a serious and disabling injury. It requires immediate attention if the disability is to be kept at a minimum and the possibility of a permanently weakened ankle avoided. Anyone can tell if they have a sprained ankle, but to know how it should be treated you need professional advice. Most sprains can be treated successfully by using proper support and restriction of weight bearing for at least the first 48 hours. Some sprains require surgical repair if the ankle is ever going to be stable, and only a physician can tell you which one that will be. The initial treatment should be application of cold, as an icebag or coldpack, and elevation to keep swelling down as a result of continued internal bleeding. This is followed by support with a plastic air splint. When the dancer is able to resume activity on that foot and leg is determined by the degree of local swelling, tenderness over the torn ligaments and ability to bear weight without pain. Since dancing with an air splint is difficult, if not impossible, the use of a canvas support or taping by a qualified therapist or trainer should continue until the sprain is healed, and this should be around the clock, not just when dancing.

The other serious ankle injuries are due to repeated contacts between the lower ends of the tibia and soft tissues and tarsal bones on the dorsum and the posterior aspects of the foot. These are called anterior and posterior impingements. Ballet dancers suffer most from these stresses because of the extremes of flexion and extension of the foot on the ankle in assuming the *demi-pointe* and *pointe* positions.

On the dorsum of the foot the joint capsule is stretched in full flexion of the foot and pinched in extension. There is pressure exerted on the neck of the talus by the anterior lip of the tibia and on the inner aspect of the talus by the medial malleolus of the tibia. Over time small bony fragments (exostoses) appear and these become painful and tender and may prevent a full range of motion.

Behind the ankle the posterior tubercle of the talus may be broken off, and if the fragment is large enough to maintain itself may be called the os trigonum. This interferes with full flexion and causes local pain and tenderness.

These exostoses may cause so much trouble that the dancer is unable to perform. Local treatment, including taking the non-steroidal anti-inflammatory drugs, may be of little help. Local injections of corticosteroids provide temporary relief at best and may only aggravate the situation. Surgical excision and repair of the capsule and some attention to the talus may help to restore useful function for several years or more, but recurrence is common.

Leg

The most common injuries to the dancer's legs involve the muscles and tendons, but stress fractures of the tibia and fibula occur and must be kept in mind when considering the aches and pains that appear to involve only the soft tissues. Superficial abrasions and contusions are more common in modern dance where some work is done on the floor.

Pain that seems centered along the tibia and going through the center of the leg is often called shin splints because of its location. It is most apt to occur when a dancer is beginning to dance or resuming dance after a long layoff. It is due to inflammation, and sometimes small tears, in the fascial covering of the long flexor muscles of the foot and perhaps also to inflammation of the periosteum of the tibia where the muscles are attached. Pain tends to be worse at rest and relieved by activity. Soaking the legs in hot water or in a whirlpool may offer some relief.

Pain deep in the leg muscles and accompanied by swelling that appears only during or immediately following dancing is usually due to what is called compartment syndrome. The strong fascia that covers and divides the muscles separates them and the accompanying blood vessels and nerves into four groups in the leg, called compartments because they may be completely enclosed. When muscle sizes increase as the result of vigorous and repeated exercise in dance the fascia may not stretch correspondingly. As the muscles swell during activity the compartment becomes too small to contain them and the circulation of the muscles is temporarily reduced or completely cut off, causing pain. Rest and elevation will give relief, but on resumption of dancing pain will recur. Physicians and trained therapists can determine whether this situation requires surgical relief by determining the pressure on the four compartments at rest and during exercise using a wick and a manometer. If the pressure differences are great enough to threaten the life of the muscles and the dancer's ability to cope a surgeon can provide relief by opening and partially removing fascia from the compartment involved.

Recurring and persistent pain in the leg in the experienced dancer accompanied by localized tenderness over either the tibia or fibula but no swelling of the leg requires x-ray examination to see whether a stress fracture is present. If plain x-ray shows nothing, a bone scan x-ray or ultrasound imaging may be necessary to see the fracture.

Rest, complete or modified, is necessary to allow a stress fracture to heal. It will take weeks and perhaps months rather than days for this to happen. The use of electrical stimulation by an implant to speed the process is still experimental. Bone grafting has been done in some resistant cases but would not be a practical solution for a dancer.

Knee

It helps in trying to understand the injuries to dancers' knees and what can be done to prevent or treat them if you know what the structures in the knee are, how they relate to each other and what roles they play in knee function, particularly in dancing. The knee is not an organ in itself but a junction between three bones—the femur, tibia and fibula—surmounted in front by a sesamoid bone, the patella, which gives the knee its characteristic appearance.

The thigh bone (femur) is held to the leg bone (tibia) and fibula by ligaments externally and internally, although it is also supported by muscles that cross the joint and the tendon of the quadriceps muscle group, which lies in front of the knee and contains the kneecap (sesamoid patella). The knee is not a simple hinge joint but has a helical motion. In the process of flexion and extension of the leg on the thigh, the thigh moves forward and backward on the leg and also rotates. This complex motion makes it possible to do many things, including dance, which would otherwise be impossible. It also operates within such narrow limits of tolerance that if one element is damaged or not functioning properly it may start a cascade of problems with other elements.

Critical elements inside the joint are the two menisci, flattened discs of fibrocartilage that assist the tibia to accommodate the motions of the prominent lower condyles of the femur, which rest on them and act as shock absorbers as well as guides. These menisci, medial and lateral, are attached to the tibia at their margins but are centrally mobile. They also attach to the medial and lateral ligaments that cross the knee outside the joint. These menisci may be torn when a foot is planted and the body and thigh turn suddenly toward one side or the other, an action that occurs frequently in dance. This is usually painful and the injury is accompanied soon after by some secretion of synovia from the lining of the knee joint. In the days following the injury weight bearing on that leg is very painful and dancing impossible.

Tears of the menisci heal poorly, if at all, because they have poor circulation, and even that may be compromised by the injury. The orthopedic surgeon will take x-rays of the knee and look into the joint with an arthroscope to determine the nature and extent of the tear. The meniscus must be preserved for the future function of the knee, in whole or at least in part. Some tears can be repaired even through the arthroscope. Completely fragmented menisci must usually be removed if they can't be reattached successfully. If the whole meniscus has to be removed, the normal motion of the knee is disturbed and eventually there will be wearing away of some of the cartilage lining the upper end of the tibia and increased risk of damage to the remaining meniscus.

Two important internal ligaments cross each other as they run from the front to the back of the knee, the anterior and posterior cruciate ligaments. Both are important in stabilizing the knee, but of the two the anterior is more so. This ligament is torn more frequently in male than female dancers because they do so much more work in lifting and turning with their partners with one leg as the base. When this ligament is torn the dancer can usually feel it internally as a sharp crack or snap. There is usually sharp pain and rapid swelling of the knee joint. If the joint is aspirated fresh blood will be found. This is an absolute emergency and the dancer should be taken directly to a hospital, preferably by ambulance and on a stretcher.

If a dancer with a torn cruciate ligament wishes to continue as a dancer it is necessary to have the ligament repaired. It may be possible for the orthopedic surgeon to repair it directly, but this usually requires a graft either to bring the ends together and reinforce them or to replace the ligament entirely. The loss of a posterior cruciate ligament is also serious, but may be easier to compensate for and more easily repaired.

The external ligaments, called the medial and lateral collateral ligaments, may be strained by dancers in a variety of movements. They are seldom torn completely through in female dancers, although sometimes in males. The strain of these ligaments is painful and temporarily disabling. The knee should be seen by a physician to establish the diagnosis. Treatment will require modified rest and support, which may be some type of brace but seldom a cast (which may allow atrophy of the thigh muscles). Surgical repair may be required where there is a complete rupture of the ligament. That injury is sometimes associated with a tear of the adjacent meniscus.

Pain in and around the kneecap or patella is a common occurrence in dancers. The patella is, and needs to be, a rather unstable sesamoid bone. It is more unstable in women than in men for several reasons. The principal one is that in women the femur makes a greater angle in joining the tibia because of their wider pelvis. This allows a strong contraction of the thigh muscles when the knee is bent and a greater chance of pulling the patella out of its natural groove between the two condyles at the lower end of the femur. Another reason is that in men the muscles on the front of the thigh, the quadriceps, are better developed and exert more stabilization. A third reason that relates particularly to dancers is the fact that so many have what is sometimes called "back knee" or in medical terms "genu recurvatum." We don't know whether this is a result of learning dance technique or whether those with this tendency make better dancers, but it does increase instability. Also, the turn-out position requires an increased external rotation of the tibia, which has a similar effect on the patella.

The patella is lined with cartilage on its inner surface and is quite sensitive to chronic irritation. The soft structures attaching to and surrounding it also become sensitive from chronic strain. The result of all this shifting around and rubbing of the cartilage on the femoral condyle is pain. When this proceeds for some time the cartilage may begin to wear down and fragment, exposing the bone, which may also erode. This is called chondromalacia and is a late stage of this process.

The tendency of the patella to slide out of its groove and to lock temporarily before slipping back in is called subluxation. This may result one day in a complete dislocation of the patella, which is very painful and makes the knee look as if it were completely dislocated. It is usually easily returned to its groove but it is a final warning that something needs to be done to prevent a recurrence. The usual treatment to relieve pain and prevent subluxation is progressive resistance exercise to strengthen the quadriceps muscle, working in the range from 20° of flexion to full extension. The dancer can continue to dance, perhaps with an elastic support to hold the patella in place. In more severe cases surgical treatment may be necessary, disabling the dancer for several months.

Thigh

The major thigh injury problem for the dancer is the deep muscle bruise, a strain of the quadriceps, sometimes called a "charley horse" for reasons that are obscure. This is painful and disabling. If not properly treated it can lead to permanent disability from dancing. The initial treatment should be external application of cold to minimize internal bleeding, application of a pressure wrap and elevation. No weight bearing should be allowed for at least the first day.

If there has not been a major tear of the muscle it is necessary to begin stretching the muscle which is in spasm after the first day. Gentle stretching, followed by voluntary contraction, is started every two hours. Elastic bandaging is maintained and limited weight bearing started. Often by the end of a week a regular schedule of dancing can be started, but still using elastic bandaging on the thigh. This is not removed until pain and swelling are completely gone and range of movement has returned to normal.

Hip

Turn-out is a rotation outward of the whole lower extremities from the hip to the toes performed in the erect position. It is a movement found in all forms of dance, although in its extreme degree in ballet. Its purpose may have originally been instinctive, as a means of preparing the body to move quickly in any direction. It has survived perhaps as a means of implying movement, even when movement does not occur, and displaying the leg in a more attractive profile.

In the average child the angle that the neck of the thigh bone (femur) makes with the hip bone as it comes out of its socket (acetabulum) is sharply down and slightly forward. As the child grows naturally the forward rotation increases and the angle of the femur towards the ground tends more toward a right angle. Around age 11 the angulation in both directions becomes stable. What happens as this takes place is that ability to rotate the femur outward decreases a great deal. If the child has not been practicing turn-out from an early age it becomes more difficult as the three strong ligaments that hold the head of the femur in the acetabulum become stronger and tighter. Girls, who start dance training usually several years before this age, can maintain their turn-out fairly well, but boys, who usually start at or after this age, can develop only a very small amount of turn-out.

One result of this situation is that young dancers who have lost the opportunity to turn out naturally injure the hip joint by forcibly stretching the supporting ligaments, injuring the internal cartilage of the joint and sometimes causing little growths of new bone on the head or neck of the femur. Attempting to force the hip may also injure the ligaments and cartilage of the knee and ankle.

To some extent such injuries can be prevented, or at least limited, by the dancer performing regularly a series of exercises to improve flexibility and preserve a good range of joint motion by stretching and moving the muscles and ligaments of the lower back, thigh and leg.

The most important overuse injury of the hip is a stress fracture, and it is usually in the neck of the femur. This is an incomplete fracture because the bone does not separate. Pain at first is mild and is felt in the groin. It is usually felt as class begins, tends to decrease during class and then to recur when class is over. As time goes on the pain becomes more persistent, although it may stop completely if the dancer is laid off. The pain will return when dancing starts again. Pain is worse at the limits of motion in all ranges, and can be reproduced with the dancer sitting or lying supine by bringing the femur across the opposite one in and rotating it inward. If the dancer continues to dance without rest or treatment the fracture will often become complete, with collapse of the hip, a tragic circumstance. The only treatment then is to reduce the fracture and insert a metal screw to hold it in place. Shortening of the extremity may occur in spite of this and the end of a dance career is almost certain. Plain x-ray may reveal the fracture, but for early detection, leading to earlier treatment and healing, a radio-isotope bone scan is a necessity. CAT scan and magnetic resonance imaging (MRI) can usually find the fracture but are much more expensive. Once the diagnosis is made all weight bearing on that leg must be substantially reduced or eliminated entirely. The dancer is put on crutches and given anti-inflammatory medication by mouth. Barre exercise can be carried out in a pool with water supporting the affected limb and conditioning maintained with one-legged cycling and upper extremity exercises. The minimum time for complete healing of the bone is about six months.

Injury to the cartilage lining the socket (acetabulum) of the hip joint may occur instead of (or in addition to) a stress fracture. If it is an ostechondral (bone and cartilage together) injury you may be able to see the bone fragment on the x-ray. If the separation of the bone is minimal it may heal with rest but if more than 1/4 inch the fragment will probably have to be removed surgically or replaced and fixed at the site from which it was fractured. Pain resembles in its occurrence and severity that of a stress fracture.

There are four groups of muscles that control movements of the femur around the hip in flexion, extension, abduction (reaching out) and adduction (pulling in). All of these muscles and their tendons can be injured as a result of an acute or a chronic strain. Acute muscle strains occur most frequently near the point of origin of the muscle from the bone and injuries of the tendon near the point of attachment. Partial or complete tears of the muscle usually happen when a sudden vigorous contraction of the muscle belly takes place that is not opposed by an equally strong contraction of the opposing muscle, or where a very strong muscle opposes a very weak one. These injuries, when only partial, cause a painful spasm of the muscle and must be treated from the outset with gentle stretching of the muscle to relieve the spasm and prevent permanent shortening.

If the tear of a muscle belly is very extensive or complete the muscle covering (fascia) must be sutured surgically. Bleeding can be controlled by tying arteries and veins. The evacuation of large blood clots will relieve pain and speed healing. This type of injury should never be massaged after bleeding has been controlled because such action may provoke the formation of calcium deposits (myositis ossificans), causing chronic fibrosis and muscle shortening.

Two strong flexors of the thigh on the hip are the iliacus and psoas muscles, which lie close together as they come beneath the inguinal ligament to insert on the lesser trochanter on the inside of the femur. The iliopsoas tendon—the combination of the two muscles—may be chronically irritated in the unfolding action of the femur as it is raised from the floor, an action called *développé* in ballet although it is common to all forms of dance. In its chronic state this will produce stiffness in the hip and often a feeling of crepitus or grating. Treatment is by modified rest, anti-inflammatory medication and developing better flexibility.

There are two bursas in the hip joint that may become inflamed and cause pain and disability. The one more commonly involved lies over the greater trochanter of the femur, the part of the bone that you feel when you press over the hip joint. It lies under the iliotibial band, a ligament very important in controlling and stabilizing the hip joint. In dancers this ligament and the bones take a great strain in landing from any jumping action, or in ballet performing the circular motion of the foot called a *rond de jambe*.

When this bursa is inflamed the dancer will feel a sharp pain from any motion that rubs or compresses it. Fluid may form in the bursa, producing a swelling that is tender and can be felt and seen. Calcium may also be deposited in the bursa, which can make it more painful. Treatment involves use of an anti-inflammatory medicine by mouth, aspiration of any fluid present and replacement by a corticosteroid. In chronic cases, especially with calcium deposits, the bursa may have to be removed surgically.

The other bursa, which lies over the anterior of the hip beneath the iliopsoas tendon, may become inflamed when the tendon does. This causes pain in the groin and may likewise be associated with a feeling of grating or crackling. Like the pain of stress fracture it may decrease during class and return after it is over. Anti-inflammatory medicine, stretching exercises and correction of poor technique will all help in recovery.

Ballet dancers sometimes complain of feeling and hearing a click as they return from *développé* to the first position. This is due to the iliopsoas tendon coming back over the anterior hip capsule. It does not cause pain unless it is present with bursitis over the anterior capsule.

Snapping hip comes from the outside of the hip and may be accompanied by a sound the dancer can hear as well as feel. It is due to the tendon of tensor fascia lata snapping forward over the greater trochanter of the femur as a ballet dancer performs a *grand plié* or lands from a leap. The action can be strong enough to cause a jerking forward of the hip, not far, but enough to spoil a graceful line. If it is due to lack of conditioning of the muscles that move the thigh away from the body (abductors) strengthening them and working on correct technique may help. If it is painful and persistent surgical division of the fascial tendon at that point may be necessary.

Pain in the back of the hip usually occurs only in older dancers and seems to be due to years of stretching the external rotators and abductors as well as the posterior capsule of the hip joint. Physical therapy, including exercises to improve flexibility, may be the only successful recourse for treatment. It may terminate a dancer's career.

Spine

The lower (lumbar) spine is the portion that is most commonly affected by injury or becomes for other reasons a source of pain and disability in dancers. It is also unfortunately the area in which it is most difficult to get everyone from the dancer, teacher, dancer director, physical therapist, choreographer to the physician to agree on the cause or origin of the problem. The best that can be done here is to point out the possible sources of trouble so that they may serve as clues to the nature of your particular problem.

The first thing to remember is that nothing comes from nothing. When the dancer's back starts to hurt, no matter how recently or whatever event brought it to his or her attention, it may not be the first time, and the cause may be directly related to that first time, if you can get back to it. That is borne out by years of experience in asking persons with low back pain if they have ever had it before. The usual reply is "only the usual morning low backache." Is low backache usual for everyone in the morning? Of course it isn't. With further questioning you can usually get back to the fall off the bicycle, the automobile accident, the heavy lifting accident or even the fall down stairs. Many of these events occur in childhood, adolescence or early adult life. If they were not unusually dramatic they are aften repressed or forgotten. Frequently a physician was not seen and no diagnosis was made.

It helps to know something more about the anatomy of the spine than you probably learned in school. It is composed of a series of bones shaped somewhat like blocks varying from relatively small sizes in the neck to large in the lumbar spine and sacrum, which make up the back portion of the pelvis. These blocks have arms that protrude to the rear of the body forming a canal that contains the spinal cord and its membranes and uniting to form a series of protrusions that form what we can see and feel as the spine. These arms fit into those above and below them in what we call articulations. The sacral bones are ordinarily fused together but have a small bony tail called the coccyx, made up of small bones firmly but not rigidly attached to the sacrum. The whole bony structure with the fibrocartilage and ligaments that hold it together are called the spinal column. The fibrocartilage is distributed between the bodies of the vertebral bones, except for the sacrum and coccyx, and helps to make a smooth articulation between these bones possible as well as serves as a shock absorber. These disks, as they are called, enable you to bend your spine forward, backward and sideways without damaging your spinal cord and the nerves that come from it and pass out through it to serve the body.

A chain is as strong as its weakest link. The spinal column has many links and is the central supporting structure of the body. The weight of the body above the pelvic girdle is borne by the spine, and if it becomes weak at some point the strain of that weight produces pain and loss of normal function. Although some pain in the lower back can be due to direct injury to a muscle or its fascial covering, the majority of serious and disabling back pain can be traced back to a problem in the structure of the spine. The muscle spasm is secondary to that problem, not primary.

The structural problems of the spine have one of two possible origins and sometimes, unfortunately, a combination of both. The first is in the defective formation of one or more of the bones in this very complex structure, and the second is in an injury to some part of one or more of the vertebra. The principal defect occurs when the arms of the vertebra fail to unite to form the posterior spines. This is called spina bifida (which means that instead of a single spine there are two incomplete and widely separated spines). When this involves more than one vertebra it can be associated with severe deformities of the spinal cord and its coverings and cause paresis (weakness) or complete paralysis below that level in the newborn. More commonly it involves only one, usually the fifth, or last, lumbar vertebra or the first sacral. Often it is not recognized early in life unless by x-ray examination of that part of the body for some other reason since it does not produce pain or disability in the early years of life. Because this failure to develop involves also the parts of those vertebra that articulate with the adjacent vertebra, this makes a weak link in the chain, which makes these vertebrae unstable.

The ligaments that hold the vertebrae together can make up for this instability, if it is not severe, during the early years of life. As the body grows larger and heavier and the ligaments become stretched by increasing activity, instability appears. Eventually, under the severe and repeated strain that occurs in dancing, traction or pressure on the spinal nerves or inflammation at the points of articulation of the spine produces pain.

The net result of all this is that starting in late adolescence young persons with unstable spines begin to experience low back pain under stress. Most often they are told it is just a muscle strain and they should rest and avoid activities that produce this strain. Rarely do they have x-rays of the lower spine, and if they do they don't always have the right views made to demonstrate the defects that cause the instability. Even if these views are made the x-rays are often reported as "normal" even when a spina bifida is clearly shown. These defects are not correctable and in the majority of cases the instability is not severe enough to require a spinal fusion.

What needs to be done is to explain the cause of the lack of stability and to show the dancer how this may be compensated by strengthening supporting muscles and correcting posture to avoid perpetuating the strain that produces the pain. The dance teacher may feel that a moderate forward curvature of the lower spine may be pleasing aesthetically, but what the person with an unstable spine needs is to keep the lower spine as straight as possible by maintaining a forward rotation of the pelvis in standing, walking, dancing and sitting.

Another type of defect that the dancer is not born with but that arises during the process of growth and can be a cause of low back pain is having a short lower extremity (thigh, leg and foot taken together). This may be discovered because of the presence of a lateral curvature in the spine (scoliosis). Seen from the rear the crest of the pelvic girdle will be higher on one side than the other. The length of the two lower extremities is measured from the anterior superior spine of the ilium to the lower border of the medial malleolus (ankle bone). The difference can be made up by using a heel lift in the shoe on the shorter side. The dancer must wear proper street shoes to make this effective and avoid the use of slippers, jazz shoes and worn down running shoes.

The second major category is instability due to spinal injury. The most common of these is a fracture in the portion of the vertebra that connects the upper and lower facets that articulate with the vertebrae above and below the injured one. This defect is called spondylolysis. Many years ago it was thought that this defect was congenital but we know now that when a section of bone is missing there it is due to an old fracture where the bone has been absorbed. These fractures occur commonly in the early years of life (ages four to eight) but are usually not recognized until years later when back pain appears due to instability and x-rays are made. The fracture may occur, however, after the young person has started to dance, either from that activity, gymnastics or other sports. If it is found early after it occurs the bone may be allowed to heal by placing the youngster in a spinal brace for a period of anywhere from three to six months.

If this defect occurs on both sides of a single vertebra, especially in the last lumbar vertebra, the lumbar spine may slip forward, a condition that is called spondylolisthesis. This condition can be classified according to the amount of forward slipping from the least (first degree) to the greatest (third degree). Those who have second degree may be able to get along with posture correction and a back support, but beyond that a spinal fusion is usually necessary to control pain and prevent associated degenerative damage.

Other fractures of the lumbar spine are possible in dancers but are rare. A compression fracture of the body of the vertebrae might occur as the result of a fall or bad landing from a high leap in a male dancer or a hard landing from a lift in a female, particularly if she suffers from some general loss of bone substance (osteoporosis), as some dancers do because of poor nutrition and hormonal changes.

A common muscle source of pain and disability in the lower back of dancers is excessive tightness and loss of strength in the psoas muscle on either or both sides. This muscle has its origins from all the lumbar vertebrae on their lateral and anterior aspects and inserts on the inner side of the femur. Its principal function is to flex the thigh at the hip and rotate the femur inward. The results of psoas tightness are inability to extend the hip with restricted turn-out, increase in lumbar lordosis with forward pelvic tilt, weakness of the abdominal muscles and tightness of the hamstrings. The dancer feels tightness and pain in the lower back on any movements in that direction such as *arabesque*, and may develop muscle strain in the shoulders as the result of a secondary forward flexion of the upper spine to balance the increased lordosis. Treatment involves selective stretching of tight muscles and strengthening of weak muscles to restore normal body alignment.

Rupture of a lumbar intervertebral disk occurs more commonly in the male ballet dancer due to lifting his partner but is not common among other dance injuries. The characteristic symptom is pain in the lower back with radiation along the course of the sciatic nerve and its branches into the lower extremity on one or both sides. Pain can be relieved only by lying down on the side with the thighs flexed on the pelvis. Once the disk has ruptured the condition will not correct itself, even with prolonged rest, and it is not possible to continue dancing effectively and without pain, although some have tried to do so. The only effective treatment is removing the ruptured disk either by surgery or by dissolving it by injection of a special enzyme.

Injuries to the spine of the upper back (thoracic) and neck (cervical) are uncommon in ballet except among the male dancers who perform lifts of partners. These are chiefly muscle strains or ligament sprains and require chiefly local application of heat followed by massage and stretching and correction of poor technique. The rhomboid muscles that hold the shoulder blades (scapula) to the chest wall are often weak and easily strained by repeatedly reaching forward and out and lifting. Male dancers should work on development of upper body and shoulder strength to prevent this.

More severe strains and sprains occur in modern and jazz dancing where vigorous and even violent movements are encouraged by the choreography, and where at times the entire body is supported by the head, neck and arms. Stiffness in the neck muscles is a common result, which requires mobilization of upper spine as well as the neck following local application of heat and massage.

Of injuries to the shoulder probably the most common is inflammation of the supraspinatus tendon, which runs across the top of the scapula to attach to the humerus. This is chiefly an overuse injury, is very painful and may prevent raising the arm above the level of the shoulder. There is also a bursa lying between the tendon and the acromion process of the scapula. When both are inflamed this is sometimes called the impingement syndrome. Treatment is rest with the arm supported by a sling and local application of cold and anti-inflammatory medicine by mouth. There is frequently weakness of other shoulder muscles. Prevention depends on strengthening the muscles.

The three muscles whose tendons come around the back of the shoulder to strengthen the capsule and provide outward rotation of the shoulder are called the rotator cuff. Partial tears of this cuff occur in lifting or in partially supporting the body on the arm in male dancers. This will cause weakness and a tendency of the head of the humerus to partially slip out of the joint in back. If not treated these tears become larger and eventually disabling. Surgical repair will allow the dancer to return to full activity.

Complete dislocations of the shoulder are unusual in dancers. Treatment requires rest and support of the arm in a sling for from three to six weeks. A second recurrence of a dislocation usually means that a surgical repair is necessary to avoid further disability.

Separation of the outer end of the clavicle from the acromion of the scapula is a painful and temporarily disabling injury. If it is a first degree sprain without appreciable separation it will heal with rest. A second degree will usually also heal, but leaves an unsightly protrusion. A third degree or complete separation will heal, but with a marked deformity and some weakness of the shoulder.

Lateral pain and tenderness over the elbow (tennis elbow) may come from repeated handstands or lifts. It is relieved by rest and anti-inflammatory medicine. Often there is weakness in muscles of the arm and forearm and they must be strengthened to prevent recurrence. Repeated recurrence may require surgical treatment.

Sprains of the wrist occur chiefly from lifts or movements in which the body is partly supported on one hand or completely on both hands. They will respond to wrist supportive strapping and anti-inflammatory medicine.

Dislocations of the carpal bones or fractures of the metacarpals are usually accidental injuries from contact with objects or another dancer.

Fractures and dislocations of the fingers are not uncommon, especially in male dancers. They must be reduced and held in place until healing occurs in six to eight weeks. Surgical repair is seldom necessary.

Head injuries are uncommon in ballet and relatively rare in modern and jazz dance. A concussion is an event signifying that an injury to the brain has occurred. It is not necessarily accompanied by any recognizable loss of consciousness, but only a feeling of being dazed and momentarily confused. Any dancer who has suffered a concussion should not continue dancing on that day but should be examined by a physician and observed to determine the nature and severity of the brain injury. Most will make an uneventful recovery, but headaches may start any time after the injury and persist for hours or days. It is better not to resume dancing until they have disappeared.

11

REHABILITATION FROM DANCE INJURIES

Objectives and Goals

Whether an illness or injury has caused a dancer to stop dancing entirely for a short or long time or has simply forced him or her to reduce the workload, his or her mind should be set on getting back to normal activity as soon as possible. Rehabilitation describes that process in brief, but doesn't specify what it means in terms of objectives, methods and goals and the persons who must necessarily be involved. This chapter will define these terms and identify the persons.

Since what a dancer considers to be normal in structure or function for his or her own body may be less than optimal looked at objectively, rehabilitation should mean not simply a return to the state before illness or injury but the development of the best possible physical and functional condition for that individual. If a dancer has strained or bruised a thigh muscle that was already weak, either from lack of good conditioning or a previous injury, and the thigh muscle on the opposite side is also weak, good rehabilitation means that both thighs should be reconditioned to optimal strength and function. It also means that where the dancer may have lost strength, endurance or flexibility during an enforced layoff, these factors must be restored or improved as well.

The methods best used depend on the particular circumstances of the illness or injury, on the facility, equipment and personnel available for the defined objectives and the willingness of the individual to cooperate with the proposed program of rehabilitation.

The availability of funds to provide the process should not be a part of the decision made, but it always is. The interest and ability that dance companies have in providing such services for dancers varies widely. Dancers who are not members of a company or in a university program are on their own.

The principal goal should always be to return the dancer to activity as soon as consistent with having reached the objectives of treatment, but before the stage in which the resumption of activity would cause a setback in the process of recovery. There is a point at which return is reasonably safe, though there may be disagreement between dancer, therapist and others involved as to when that point has been reached. This is a practical matter that seldom satisfies all parties, but careful monitoring of the dancer's return to activity will reveal whether the decision must be reconsidered.

Selecting the Therapist

The selection of the therapist will not always be in the hands of the dancer. Insofar as it is, the dancer's choice will be influenced by personal and family tradition, advice of supervisors and colleagues, availability and past experiences. For the treatment of an illness there is little choice except a physician. Some companies may have a nurse or some other professional who can help the dancer decide whether an indisposition has become an illness that requires a physician.

For the treatment of an injury there may be a person connected with the company or program who is qualified as a podiatrist, a physical therapist or sports trainer who can undertake the management of simple problems and can decide when the physician's advice and services are needed. It is not easy to make a distinction between minor and major injuries since every injury is of major consequence to the person who has it. If the dancer has any question as to whether a physician's help is required it should be satisfied by consulting one. In the long run it may save time and money and shorten the disability, even though it may not seem so at the time.

Any therapist should be professionally qualified by training and degree or certification. Many persons profess to dancers that they are qualified therapists, unfortunately, who have no recognized professional qualifications. Typically they offer a particular form of therapy rather than a range of services, and claim that their particular form is good for whatever the problem may be. Any person willing to believe that is willing to believe anything.

Until very recently there has been very little information about the causes, nature and appropriate treatment of dancers' injuries available to physicians. As a consequence dancers may have had difficulty in finding physicians who had a good understanding of their situation and their particular problems. The same was true years ago about the relationship between physicians and athletes. Both have learned from cultivating these relationships, and the same thing is possible for dancers.

If your company or program has a physician as their consultant he or she may specialize in a primary care area such as general practice, family medicine, internal medicine or adolescent medicine. He or she may be an orthopedic surgeon or even a gynecologist. If you have to make a choice and do not have a family physician you might start with a primary care physician rather than an orthopedic surgeon, unless you already know that your problem will require surgery.

Podiatrists have treated many dancers because foot problems are so common among them. Many companies today have a consultant podiatrist who has particular interest and experience with dancers. Podiatrists and physicians work together effectively in the management of dancers' problems.

Physical therapists are frequently associated with dance companies and provide conditioning as well as therapeutic services. The therapist who has worked with dancers may be specially qualified to determine how faulty techniques that contribute to injuries may be corrected by specific training exercises.

Persons who have had specific training in kinesiology and biomechanics can also contribute to injury prevention among dancers and may be very important consultants in the process of rehabilitation.

Establishing the Program

The process of rehabilitation should be continuous from the time that therapy begins. There should be no letup in maintaining the general conditioning of the body and the function of the uninjured parts. It also means that every step in the process is part of a coordinated chain which is connected with the succeeding steps to reach the desired goal. As far as the dancer is concerned it is an active rather than a passive process.

Each step should be in a logical progression so that it builds on the preceding steps to move smoothly towards the stated goal. If surgical treatment is part of the program physical therapy may be appropriate before as well as after the surgery. Psychological counseling for adapting to the particular surgery should begin before the surgery. Improvement of nutritional practices, if necessary, should not have to wait until the treatment of the strained Achilles tendon has finished. This requires careful scheduling by the dancer as well as the concerned therapist.

If the dancer is completely disabled it may be easier to arrange the program of rehabilitation and will make it possible to devote the entire day to the necessary activities. If cold or heat applications are necessary, they may be more effective if they can be four times a day rather than once or twice. Time conflicts can be avoided and a greater variety of activities scheduled.

If the dancer is to continue to work on a limited basis appointments for therapy have to be arranged at non-conflicting times. This is easier if the principal therapist is part of the company or institution and knows the regular schedules. The company director must be kept informed but at the same time must approve reasonable arrangements that require the dancer to miss some regularly scheduled activities. If the therapist is not a regular consultant or a member of the company, scheduled appointments will have to be made when the company does not have specific activities.

The program typically will consist of evaluation of status and progress by the therapist, sessions of therapeutic and rehabilitative exercise, general conditioning and counseling regarding injury prevention, nutrition and possible changes in technique. Some of these sessions will take place only once a week or less and others every day. The program should be arranged so that there is not too much concentration in one day and so that the dancer can be kept busy when not involved in a modified dance activity.

How Long Will It Take?

It will take as long as is necessary to accomplish the stated goals for the dancer. In one case this will be a week and in another six months. Trying to shortcut rehabilitation is the best way to prevent complete rehabilitation and to set the stage for a recurrence or another related problem. What may appear an immediate gain for the professional dancer may turn into a long-term loss.

Damaged and surgically treated tissues take time to heal. The amount of time depends on the nature, extent and location of the damage, and to some extent on whether there has been previous damage in the same area and on the age and general physical condition of the injured person. There are no such persons as "fast healers" or "slow healers" if other factors are not present. It is practically impossible to infect a clean healed incision after seven days but it may be possible to disrupt the skin after even three weeks. A fractured bone may show evidence of healing by x-ray in four to six weeks, but it may not be healed sufficiently to prevent refracture in the same place before six months.

The dancer should be ready to accept the decision of the therapist as to when he or she is ready to resume full activities, including performance. The experienced dancer can often tell but the inexperienced one may be afraid even when things appear to be going well.

12

PREVENTION OF DANCE INJURIES

The tragic tale of Achilles in ancient Greek mythology is one of the earliest lessons in injury prevention (Abel's need for protective headgear is also a good one). According to Homer's *Iliad*, Achilles was the offspring of Peleus and the sea goddess Thetis, the leader of the Myrmidons; pretty good genes to start with. Thetis, as mothers will, wanted to protect her only son from any harm, so she grabbed the infant Achilles by the right heel and dipped him in some magic waters—right up to his fateful heel. This waterproofing supposedly protected Achilles from mortal injury. As an adult, Achilles became the hero of the siege of Troy, and avenged the murder of his best friend by slaying Hector, the son of the King of Troy, and having Hector's carcass dragged around Troy. Later, Achilles met his match when Paris, Hector's brother, discovered Achilles' only fatal flaw, and shot him in the heel.

Although Achilles' injuries may not be physically fatal, they certainly can and have been professionally fatal. Relatively minor irritations of a tendon along with a childish denial of its significance ("it will be better in the morning") ripen into intractable scars. It is unbelievable how many dance-related injuries are preventable and inexcusable.

The dancer's "Achilles heel" is his or her reluctance to admit the need for using injury prevention techniques prior to the onset of the first injury. To do so would be an admission of vulnerability; a disturbing thought when one is preoccupied with the challenges of dance technique. A working knowledge of injury prevention principles and techniques are the "magic waters" which can assure the longevity and quality of a dancer's career. Like Achilles, this protection should start at the beginning of a dancer's career.

Responsibility of Injury Prevention

Whereas breaking the cycle of injury requires a thorough analysis of the factors which have contributed to a dance-related injury (exhibits 9-1 & 9-2), doing something about these factors requires a comprehensive and cooperative effort on the part of the company, dance profession, patrons of the dance, medical and health professionals, and the dancer (exhibit 12-1; all exhibits follow at end of chapter). All must equally share the responsibility for such a program.

The Dance Company and School

One of the primary responsibilities of the dance company and school is to nurture the artistic, physical and psychological aspects of the dancer. Every year, ballet companies waste thousands of dollars and many talented dancers, because they failed to realize the financial and artistic rewards of developing effective injury prevention programs. The company should provide this service to the dancers. Indeed, all major dance studios, pre-professional schools and university dance education programs should require training in the concepts, methods and utilization of injury prevention principles and techniques. Injury prevention should begin at the start of serious dance training, not after an injury has already occurred or a career has begun.

The Dance Profession

Many times, dancers are reluctant to protest their constant exposure to hazards while dancing. Dance unions and concerned groups of dancers must impress upon the company the need for injury prevention. If the company is not willing to listen to representatives of the dancers about their health and safety concerns, then appropriate collective action should be initiated on behalf of the dancers. These representatives should be on the front line of the battle for the rights of dancers.

Patrons of the Dance

Both the audience and society should realize that dance is a strenuous occupation, and that part of the cost of their ticket should be paying to keep the dancer healthy. Most dancers do not particularly want the audience to be preoccupied with the notion that they bear the scars of many old and new wounds. Dancers want to be viewed as performing artists rather than stoic soldiers. Nevertheless, it is in the best interest of the dancer that the audience and society develop an awareness of the health and medical concerns and needs of the dancer. A patron's ideological and financial support of dance as a meaningful occupation and important contribution to the quality of our society can be influential in encouraging the preservation of a dancer's career. Dancers need to know that the public is as concerned about their welfare as they are about their artistry.

The Medical Team

The medical team plays an important role in developing and implementing an effective injury prevention program. The basic medical team is composed of physicians, such as an internist and orthopedic surgeon, a physiotherapist and a specialist in etiology and prevention of injuries. All of these individuals share a special interest and knowledge in the healthcare of professional dancers. Other members may include a massage therapist, dietician, osteopath, psychologist, gynecologist, dentist or occupational therapist. The medical team should:

1. establish cooperation and communication between the injured dancer and the company;

2. educate the public and other health professionals about the health and medical concerns of the dancer;

3. provide essential treatment, rehabilitation and medical support for the dancers; and

4. perform research on the medical and scientific aspects of dance.

The Dancer

The ultimate responsibility for the utilization of an injury prevention program belongs to the dancer. There is ample evidence to convince the young aspiring dancer as to the critical need for preventing injuries in order to have a long career. A dancer should be taught the concepts and methods of injury prevention techniques at the earliest stages of training. However, it is very difficult to convince a young dancer the need for preventing an injury that she does not believe will ever happen. Youth is often unable to understand age and disability; yet few dancers retire because of too much good health.

The Cycle of Injury

Before you can prevent an injury you have to understand the reasons why it occurred in the first place. The cycle of injury begins with the causative factors that contributed to the injury (exhibit 12-2). Effective treatment and rehabilitation also play a role in your successful return to dancing.

A working knowledge of the causes of dance injuries is an essential prelude to the development of any effective injury prevention program. Causal factors have been discussed in detail in chapter 9 as well as in our parent book, *Dance Medicine: A Comprehensive Guide* (The Physician and Sportsmedicine and Pluribus Press: Chicago, 1987). Some examples of causative factors include: being forced to return to dancing before the completion of treatment or rehabilitation (occupational); excessive workload (training); forcing the turn-out (technique); "pigeon-toed" alignment (anatomical); tight calf muscles (biomechanical); hard stage or studio floors (environmental); caloric, protein, or electrolyte deficiencies (nutritional); and eating disorders, depression, or burn-out (psychological). Any of these situations or conditions as well as others can cause an injury. *If you have been injured while dancing, you must assess the reasons why the injury occurred.* If you don't, your chances of reinjury are extremely high.

Delay of treatment, or ineffective or abbreviated treatment or rehabilitation programs may also cause you to become reinjured. The cycle of injury and reinjury can be broken by a complete, accurate analysis of your predisposition to injury and subsequent development of safe and effective injury rehabilitation and prevention programs.

An effective injury prevention and rehabilitation program should include strengthening and stretching exercises designed to:

1. Correct muscle imbalances, especially in the hips and calves.

2. Increase range of motion of the joints of the spine and lower extremity to facilitate turn-out and extension and general flexibility.

3. Prepare the dancer to perform specific dance movements better or safer.

4. Form the basis of a safe and effective warm-up program.

5. Educate the dancer about predisposition to injury or the causes of dance injuries and how he or she can prevent them.

6. Help the dancer maintain his or her physical condition as well as aiding in the actual rehabilitation.

Injury Prevention Programs and Exercises

You should set aside time in your daily schedule to perform exercises which may enhance your ability to dance or help prevent certain types of dance-related injuries. An hour or so every morning is usually the best time to do these exercises. Ideally, soak in warm bath water for 10–15 minutes and gently massage the major muscle groups of the lower extremity (always stroking the muscles in the direction of venous return to the heart). Afterwards, you can throw on some old sweats and perform some or all of the exercises that follow.

Most of these exercises are done on the floor with a towel or mat for protection and warmth. If you don't have time to do all of each exercise, reduce the number of sets or repetitions. In this way these exercises can be a relatively quick 15–20 minute warm-up program. Try to keep the program simple, painless, and soothing, and in the same general order as listed—develop a fixed routine and stick with it.

Concentrate on the correct alignment of the body and performance of the exercise. The exercises are intended to help your dancing or your return to dancing after a minor injury. These exercises are for serious *dancers,* and are not recommended for the general public who have no need or preparation for the extreme range of motion, flexibility and strength demanded by dance technique. Even so, some dancers may find some of the exercises to be too difficult or uncomfortable to perform. Use some common sense when doing these exercises—*if it hurts, don't do it.* Ask yourself why it hurts (Are you performing the exercise correctly or is there a structural/functional problem?), and, if necessary, seek the advice of a qualified health professional.

The exercises are designed to strengthen and stretch the specific, isolated muscle groups used in dance, especially ballet. Some of the exercises may not be relevant to the needs of a particular dancer. In some cases a dancer may have a preexisting condition or injury that may preclude the performance of some of these strenuous exercises. If you have any such situation or questions, it is always wise to *check with your physician prior to utilizing these exercises.* Strengthening exercises of isolated muscle groups are followed by stretching exercises in the following sequence:

- Abdominals/back
- Internal/external rotators of the hip
- Hamstrings/quadriceps
- Superficial/deep calf
- Plantarflexors/dorsiflexors of the foot

All effective stretching techniques are based upon spinal cord reflexes. It is beyond the scope of this book to discuss in detail the neuroanatomical and neurophysiological basis of stretching exercises; nevertheless, the following exercises are based upon these scientific principles as they relate to the specific needs of a dancer. For example, slow, progressive static stretches for 30–60 seconds are used for smaller muscle groups such as the hip rotators. Ballistic or bouncy stretching techniques are not used in any of these exercises.

Contract/relax stretching techniques, also called proprioceptive neuromuscular facilitation (PNF), are quite effective for stretching the hamstrings, groin muscles, and quadriceps. These exercises take advantage of the decreased muscle tension (hypotonia) that immediately follows an isometric contraction of a stretched muscle. During this hypotonic phase, the muscle can be stretched even more (see the hamstring exercise for more details).

One final principle, any effective stretching exercise requires the use of relaxation and breathing techniques. During most of these exercises, you should close your eyes, isolate the particular target muscle group, remove any anxiety associated with the exercise, relax and breathe slowly and deeply, and try to visualize the correct performance of the exercise. Relaxing or soothing music can help create a pleasant ambiance and aid in the slow progressive pacing of the exercises during a session.

Abdominal/Back Series

1. Modified Roll-ups

Dancers need firm, strong abdominal muscles to support the spine and maintain proper alignment during dance movements. Low back syndrome in professional dancers may be due to lifting a partner or an extremely high *arabesque* and is often associated with weak abdominal muscles. Low back syndrome can be prevented or minimized by specifically strengthening the rectus abdominis and internal and external obliques muscles. The modified roll-up selectively strengthens these important muscles.

To begin the modified roll-up, lie on your back with the hands either behind the head and the arms flat on the floor or the arms folded across the chest (exhibit 12-3). The hips and knees are bent at 90 degree angles. Slowly lift the torso while maintaining the elongation of the upper back and neck, hold this position for eight seconds, and then slowly roll down (exhibit 12-4). The exercise is repeated with slight twists to the right and left for the internal and external oblique muscles. The neck and arms should not flex forward during this exercise, and you should be able to breathe comfortably during this exercise. A total of 3 to 6 sets are performed.

2. Modified Cobra Stretch

After the roll-up exercises, the abdominal muscles are very warmed up, fatigued and tight. It is necessary to stretch these muscles to encourage blood flow and minimize muscle soreness. The cobra stretch starts with the dancer prone, hands beneath the shoulders, and the legs in a slight second position. The abdominal muscles are stretched by gently raising the torso and keeping the hips on the floor (exhibit 12-5). Be careful while performing the cobra, and concentrate on gradual stretching of the abdominal muscle and flexibility of the spine. You should do two or three repetitions of 20–30 seconds each. This exercise is not recommended if you have back problems.

3. Modified Back Extensions

This three-part exercise is an effective strengthening exercise for the low back (erector spinae) muscles. These muscles aid in supporting the torso during certain dance movements such as *arabesque*. Once again, avoid these back exercises if you have any problems with your lower back.

It begins with the dancer supine, arms in fifth position *en haute* and the legs in a slight second position with the feet pointed and turned-out (exhibit 12-6). Slowly lift the torso and hold this position for eight seconds, and then relax (exhibit 12-7). During this part of the exercise, keep the arms properly placed, shoulders relaxed (no shrugging), and the shoulder blades flat. The arms must not pull backwards (no "dying swans").

In the second part of this exercise, gradually raise your legs (keeping your legs turned-out and the toes pointed, of course), hold for eight seconds, and slowly lower (exhibit 12-8). Finally, slowly lift both the torso and legs (remembering the previous precautions), hold for eight seconds, and lower (exhibit 12-9). To balance the effects of the modified roll-ups, do three to six sets of the back series.

4. Lumbar Roll

Lying on your back, lift the right thigh (knee bent) up to hip level, and gently stretch it across the body to the left for about 30 seconds (exhibit 12-10). Repeat with the left leg. This helps to stretch the lumbar and oblique muscles.

5. Passé *Stretch.*

Sit up from the lumbar roll into the *passé* stretch with the right leg in *passé* and the right hand on the knee (exhibit 12-11). Slowly press forward, keeping your back flat and legs turned-out. This position is held for about 30 seconds, then change sides. This exercise stretches the muscles of the lower back, hip and posterior thigh depending upon which one is tightest.

Hip Series

Hip Stretches

1. Knock-kneed Stretch for the Turn-out Muscles

The internal rotation of the knock-kneed stretch specifically stretches the external rotator muscles of the hip, which are used in turning-out. Lie on your back with your knees bent and feet separated about three feet (exhibit 12-12). The knees are brought together with slight pressure, but should not touch each other. Hold for 20–30 seconds. Then release the left leg, allow the right leg to press towards the floor, and gently fold the left knee towards the right (exhibit 12-13). This is repeated on the left side. The stretch is maintained for 20–30 seconds in each of the three positions.

If you have any pain on the medial (inner) aspect of the knee, try straightening your legs a little bit. The knock-kneed and diamond stretches are performed after each exercise in the following hip series. At the conclusion of the hip series you may notice considerable improvement in the smoothness and symmetry of movement in the hip joint as well as increased awareness and control of your turn-out.

2. Diamond Stretch

The diamond stretch should be performed while lying on your back rather than face-down. The purpose is to stretch the internal rotator muscles of the hip and the adductor (groin) muscles of the thigh, and strengthen the external rotator muscles of the hip and the peroneal (lateral) muscles of the leg.

Start with your legs flexed at the hip and knees, heels off of the floor, and the feet pointed (exhibit 12-14). Over a 30 second interval, gradually attempt to turn-out maximally while maintaining a normal curvature to the lumbar spine. Try to relax the inner thigh muscles and isolate the external rotator muscles. Keeping the feet pointed during this exercise helps to strengthen the peroneal muscles on the lateral aspect of the leg. The peroneal muscles help to bevel (abduct) the foot *en l'air* as well as oppose the action of the powerful calf (triceps surae) muscles in the *plié*.

3. Partnered Diamond Stretch

The partnered diamond exercise is an advanced stretching exercise which uses a contract/relax (PNF) technique. It is most effective when your groin (adductor) muscles are warmed-up and you're working with a trustworthy, responsible partner. You should be cautious and aware of over-stretching during this exercise.

While in the diamond position, a partner blocks your feet with his or her knees, and *gently and carefully* presses down on your knees until your groin (adductor) muscles are mildly stretched (exhibit 12-15). After 20 seconds of static stretch (do not increase the stretch during this phase), very slowly start to push your knees against the resistance of your partner's hands. Gradually increase the intensity of the contraction for six seconds, sustain a maximal contraction for about two seconds, and then relax. Your partner's initial passive stretch, followed by your isometric contraction and relaxation comprise one set of this exercise.

Your partner must be ready for the muscle relaxation and avoid applying excessive tension on your knees. A mild stretch is sufficient in this exercise, and both your partner and you need to be careful and aware of excessive amounts of tension in the groin muscles. The abdominal muscles must maintain the proper tilt of the pelvis and alignment of the lower spine during this exercise.

After 20 seconds of relaxation, the contraction can be repeated, and a total of three sets can be performed in a continuous series. Your partner should be aware that during the third set, the extremely stretched groin muscles will be able to generate very little force, and he or she should be careful not to over-stretch. It is best to do three or four sets at a lower intensity rather than one or two sets at maximal tension. At the end of this exercise your knees are slowly brought back together by your partner.

Hip Strengthening Exercises

1. Vertical Hip Rotations

Lying on our back, bend your knees, lift your thighs to hip level, and extend your legs straight up towards the ceiling (exhibit 12-16). Slowly rotate the legs inward and outward while maintaining the same vertical position of the legs. After 8–16 repetitions, bend the knees, place the feet on the floor, and perform the knock-kneed and diamond hip stretches.

2. Hip Rotations à la seconde

The same basic rotations are also performed *à la seconde*. Lying on your back, bend your knees, lift your thighs to hip level, extend your legs straight up towards the ceiling, and split *à la seconde* (exhibit 12-17). You may support the thighs with your hands if necessary. Maximally rotate the legs inward and outward for 8–16 repetitions. The legs should remain at the same height during these rotations. A change in height of the legs may indicate the presence of a muscle imbalance of the rotator muscles of the hips. After this exercise, bring the legs together, bend the knees, place your feet on the floor, and do both the knock-kneed and diamond hip stretches.

3. Leg circles à la seconde

Circumduction is a cone-shaped movement with the apex originating at one joint (usually either the hip or shoulder) and the distal extremity inscribing a circular pattern. Circumduction of the lower extremity (thigh and leg) occurs at the hip and requires a balanced synergistic coordination of the hip musculature. Irregular circular patterns may indicate the presence of a muscle imbalance of the rotator muscles of the hips, or the need for proprioceptive (position-sense) conditioning.

Lying on your back, bend your knees, lift your thighs to hip level, extend your legs straight up towards the ceiling, and split *à la seconde* (exhibit 12-17). Slowly attempt to inscribe 8–16 symmetrical 12 inch circles with the tips of your toes. Do the circles both *en dedans* and *en dehors*. After this exercise, bring the legs together, bend the knees, place your feet on the floor, and do both the knock-kneed and diamond hip stretches.

4. Développé/Enveloppé

The *développé/enveloppé* exercises are excellent for developing full range of motion at the hip, improving extension, and minimizing the occurrence of snapping and clicking noises in the hips. In the *développé* exercise the working leg moves smoothly and rhythmically from a straight position (exhibit 12-18) to flexed *en avant* (exhibit 12-19) to flexed *à la seconde à la hauteur* (exhibit 12-20), back to the fully extended position (exhibit 12-18). Notice that the non-working leg is bent in the *passé* position with the foot pointed; this protects the lower back and reinforces the proper alignment of the foot.

In the *enveloppé* exercise the working leg moves smoothly and rhythmically from a straight position (exhibit 12-18) to flexed *à la seconde à la hauteur* (exhibit 12-20) to flexed *en avant* (exhibit 12-19) and back to the fully extended position (exhibit 12-18). The non-working leg remains in the *passé* position with the foot pointed for protection of the lower back. A total of 8–16 repetitions are performed of each exercise, and then repeated on the opposite side.

If you have problems with binding or clicking noises in the hip, try this exercise with less flexion at the hip. After a couple of months of performing the hip series of exercises, the tightness and noises should be eliminated or minimized.

5. Attitude Devant

Lying on your back with the right leg in *attitude devant*, the dancer stabilizes the thigh with the right hand on the knee (exhibit 12-21). The knee is flexed 90 degrees. The leg is turned-out (exhibit 12-22) and turned-in for 8–16 repetitions in a slow swinging movement of the leg. The exercise is repeated on the left side. You should concentrate isolating the movement in the hip joint and working the full range of motion. The leg should swing in smooth arcs with the thigh providing a vertical axis of rotation. The thigh should not flex or abduct during this exercise. Avoid "sickling" the foot while turning-out during this exercise.

Hamstring Series

The hamstring series is designed to warm-up, strengthen and stretch the gluteal and hamstring muscles. They also develop the extension necessary for *arabesque* and *attitude derrière*. These exercises are performed on your hands and knees with a pad under the supporting knee. Concentrate on correct alignment of the body, placement of the leg, and turn-out. Do hamstring exercise one through three on the right side before changing sides.

1. Grande et Petite Pique à Terre en Derrière

Warm-up the hip, gluteal and hamstring musculature with 8–16 slow *grande piques,* and 8–16 fast *petite piques* (exhibit 12-23). These exercises also help reestablish proprioception in the hip joint after the hip series of exercises. Keep your head up so that visual cues about the working leg are eliminated. Make the touches to the floor very light and resilient.

2. Extend Straight Leg to Arabesque

From the kneeling position, bring your leg forward until the knee touches your forehead (exhibit 12-24), and then slowly extend the foot along the floor until it is straight (exhibit 12-23), raise the leg into the *arabesque* position (exhibit 12-25), and slowly reverse directions to the forward position (exhibit 12-24). This sequence is repeated for 8–16 repetitions. You should concentrate on turn-out and proper body alignment rather than height. Do not bend the arms, pull forward on the supporting leg, or permit the pelvis to tilt laterally.

3. Extend Attitude Derrière to Arabesque

The previous exercise can be performed in the same sequence with a slight modification. From the starting position (exhibit 12-24), to *à terre* position (exhibit 12-23), to an *attitude derrière* (exhibit 12-26), and finally extending into *arabesque* (exhibit 12-25) with a slow return to the starting position. Eight to sixteen repetitions are performed.

5. V-seat Hamstring Stretch

The hamstrings are stretched by using a modified contraction/relaxation exercise. Sit in a wide "V-seat" position with the arms fifth *en haute* and the legs slightly in front of you (exhibit 12-27). Twist to the right (exhibit 12-28), stretch over the right leg and hold that position over the leg for eight seconds (exhibit 12-29), and then release the tension and stretch the hamstring for 30 seconds. Repeat the sequence to the left.

6. Partnered Hamstring Stretch

While lying on your back, a partner supports your right leg with his or her right shoulder. Your partner *gently and carefully* applies pressure to your leg to stretch the hamstring muscles on the back of the thigh (exhibit 12-30). After 20 seconds of static stretch (do not continue to increase the stretch during this phase), very slowly start to push your right leg against the resistance of your partner's shoulder. Gradually increase the intensity of the contraction for six seconds, sustain a maximal contraction of the hamstrings and gluteal (buttock) muscles for about two seconds and then relax.

Your partner must be ready for the muscle relaxation and avoid applying excessive tension on your hamstrings or falling over on top of you (maintaining a staggered stance is important for the partner's balance). A moderate stretch is sufficient in this exercise, and both your partner and you need to be very careful and aware of excessive amounts of tension on the hamstrings.

Your partner's initial stretch, followed by your isometric contraction and subsequent relaxation comprise one set of this exercise. Three continuous sets are usually performed without releasing the stretch. By the third set the hamstrings will be so stretched that they may not be able to generate very much force; therefore, your partner should be very careful not to over-stretch. It is best to do more sets at a lower intensity than one or two sets at maximal tension. At the end of this exercise the dancer's leg is slowly returned to the floor by the partner. Repeat on the left leg.

Quadriceps Series

1. Grande et Petite Cabrioles Devant

Cabrioles are good exercises for warming-up the quadriceps muscles on the front of the thighs. The abdominal muscles must be tight during this exercise to protect the lower back and avoid over-arching the lower spine. This exercise is not recommended if you have weak abdominal muscles or lower back problems.

This exercise is performed in a semi-reclining position with your torso supported on your elbows (exhibit 12-31). Lift your legs into the *cabriole devant* position with the right leg on top, and carefully perform 8–16 slow *grande cabrioles* and 8–16 rapid *petite cabrioles devant*. Switch legs and repeat with the left leg.

2. Modified Hurdler's Stretch

While sitting, pull the right thigh out to the side, bend the left leg in front and slowly recline—gradually increasing the amount of stretch on the quadriceps on the front of the right thigh (exhibit 12-32). Hold the stretch for at least 30 seconds. Flexing the left leg allows the pelvis to rotate, and protects the lower spine by maintaining a normal curvature. Repeat the exercise on the left side.

If you feel pain on the inner side of the right knee, try straightening your right leg slightly to stabilize the knee. This complaint is quite common in dancers who force their turn-out.

Calf Series

1. Superficial Calf Stretch

The superficial calf muscles or gastrocnemius muscles are often abnormally tight in professional dancers. This condition is referred to as functional equinus and seriously predisposes the dancer to injuries of the foot, ankle and leg. Sit with your legs straight in front, reach forward and grab the feet (exhibit 12-33). Contracting the muscles on the front of your legs (tibialis anterior and extensors of the toes) at the same time you are stretching the gastrocnemius muscles seems to facilitate the stretch. Hold the stretch for 30 seconds, or three continuous sets of ten seconds, each one more intense than the previous one. Highly-active dancers should perform this exercise at least six times a day.

2. Deep Calf Stretch

In professional dancers the deep calf muscles, such as the soleus and tibialis posterior, are also too tight. The soleus is active when the knees are bent in the *demi-plié* and the tibialis posterior helps control excessive rolling-in (pronation) on the medial arch of the foot. These muscles are a bit harder to stretch than the gastrocnemius.

To stretch the deep calf muscles from the seated position, bend the right knee, place the head next to the medial side of the bent knee, grab the right foot and actively flex it (exhibit 12-34). Slowly straighten the right leg while maintaining the foot flexion and head position next to the knee. Hold the stretch for 30 seconds or three continuous sets of ten seconds, each one more intense than the previous one. Deep calf stretches should be performed as often as the superficial calf exercise.

Foot Series

1. Foot Stretch with Heel Block

Dancers perform a variety of bizarre and possibly traumatizing techniques in an effort to obtain a well-pointed foot. The safe method of stretching the foot in the pointed position is shown in exhibit 12-35. Cup the right heel in the right hand (palm up) with the thumb on top of the heel. Grasp the top of the right foot with the left hand, and gently stretch the pointed foot. Use a very firm grip on the heel to block movement of the heel and prevent it from jamming against the back of the ankle as you stretch the foot. The heel block prevents the calcaneus (heel bone) from grinding against the back of the ankle joint.

If you have straight or over-arched feet when you point, you do not need this particular stretch. If you have a poor point, you should be aware that there are limits as to how much flexibility you can force on your feet without getting injured. If you are within 10° of a full point, this foot stretch may well make up the difference. More than 15–20° short of a full point, and you're expecting too much from any reasonable exercise and you are risking the health and future of your feet.

2. Foot Exercises

The foot may be strengthened and ankle joint proprioception (position sense) enhanced by: sickling and bevelling the foot against resistance; curling up a towel beneath the toes, and spelling the alphabet by moving only the tip of the foot.

3. Hallux Manipulation

The flexibility of the hallux or big toe joint (first metatarsophalangeal joint) must be capable of dorsiflexing close to 90° to have a normal *demi-pointe* (see exhibit 9-12). You can help maintain the range of motion in this joint by applying traction to the big toe, and passively flexing, extending, adducting, abducting, and inwardly and outwardly rotating the hallux. This manipulation is most effective when the foot has been soaking in warm water.

4. Standing Demi-pointe Foot Stretch

This exercise on *demi-pointe* stretches the first metatarsophalangeal joint (big toe joint) as well as the instep of the feet. It is performed standing at the barre, and follows a sequence of *relevé, plié en demi-pointe* (exhibit 12-36), return to *demi-pointe*, and then lower to the standing position. Three to six repetitions prior to taking class are quite adequate. If you have limited range of motion of either the ankle or big toe joint, you should be careful about overstressing and irritating these areas.

Standing Stretches at the Barre

1. Standing Quadriceps Stretch

Stand facing the barre, bend your right leg and reach behind you and grab your foot with your left hand. Gently pull the leg up and back to get a moderate stretch of the front of the thigh for about 30 seconds. Release and go to the next exercise (i.e., switch sides at the end of this series of standing stretches).

2. Standing Hamstring Stretch

Stand facing the barre in a staggered stance with the left leg forward. Support your upper body with your hands on the barre. Slowly bend forward, keeping your back flat and sustain a moderate stretch in the hamstrings for about 30 seconds. Go to the next exercise.

3. Standing Deep Hip Flexor Stretch

Lean the body (*tombé*) towards the barre, maintain the pelvis in that forward position and gradually arch your torso away from the barre (exhibit 12-37). Continue to press the pelvis gently towards the barre. This exercise stretches the iliopsoas muscle, a powerful flexor of the thigh and trunk located deep in the upper front of the thigh. The iliopsoas plays a critical role in correct body alignment and the initiation of many forward movements. Release the stretch by bringing the trunk forward again, and go to the next exercise.

4. Standing Superficial Calf Stretch

In order to stretch the superficial calf muscle (gastrocnemius) simply lean towards the barre, keeping the right knee straight and right heel on the floor (exhibit 12-38). Hold for 30 seconds and go to the deep calf stretch.

5. Standing Deep Calf Stretch

Continue your calf stretches by slowly bending the right knee while leaning forward and keeping the heel on the floor (exhibit 12-

39). The deep calf muscles are active during the *demi-pliê*, and are frequently involved in overuse injuries associated with excessive jumping, hard floors and punitive work schedules. After 30 seconds release the stretch, change sides and repeat the sequence of standing stretches on the left.

Conclusion

No one can guarantee that a series of exercises will spare you from having a dance-related injury. That would be a foolish claim. But what's our alternative? Should we continue to allow the attrition of some of our best young dancers and our prized experienced professionals? Something must be done. We have learned that injury prevention is more than a series of exercises. Many scientific, medical, legal and occupational factors merge into the singular purpose of helping dancers to have long, healthy careers. To this end we share an equal responsibility to aid in the development of effective injury prevention programs and the establishment of adequate healthcare for dancers.

Injury prevention can and does work, but it takes time and money along with the belief and commitment of the majority of people in the dancer's world. Changes in the prevalence of injuries and the cost of healthcare cannot occur overnight; nevertheless they can change for the better. When injury prevention techniques are combined with a comprehensive approach to assessing and minimizing various causative factors, backed by a support team of dance and health professionals, you will see change. Imagine having an abundance of dancers who lived their dream of a long and fruitful and glorious career in dance. That's what we want and that's what we can achieve.

Exhibit 12-1
The World of the Dancer

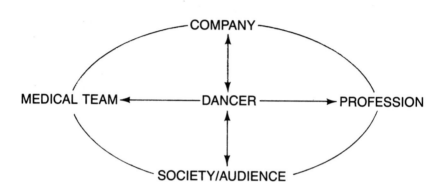

Exhibit 12-2.
The Cycle of Injury.

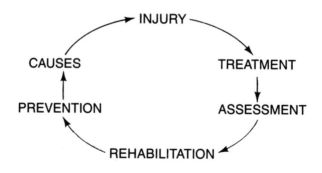

Exhibit 12-3.
Modified Roll-up Exercise (Starting position)

Exhibit 12-4.
Modified Roll-up Exercise (Up position)

Exhibit 12-5.
Cobra Stretch

Exhibit 12-6.
Modified Back Extensions (Starting position)

Exhibit 12-7.
Modified Back Extensions (Torso only)

Exhibit 12-8.
Modifed Back Extensions (Legs only)

Exhibit 12-9.
Modifed Back Extensions (Both legs & torso)

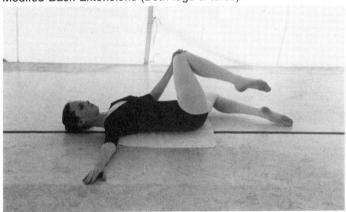

Exhibit 12-10.
Lumbar Roll

Exhibit 12-11.
Passé Stretch

Exhibit 12-12.
Knock-kneed Stretch for Turn-out Muscles (Starting position)

Exhibit 12-13.
Knock-kneed Stretch for Turn-out Muscles (Right leg only)

Exhibit 12-14.
Diamond Stretch

Exhibit 12-15.
Partnered Diamond Stretch

Exhibit 12-16.
Vertical Hip Rotations

Exhibit 12-17.
Hip Rotations *à la Seconde*

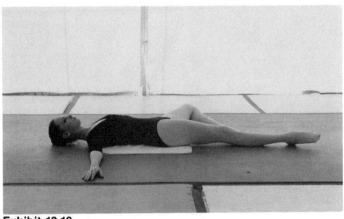

Exhibit 12-18.
Développé/Enveloppé Exercises (Starting position)

Exhibit 12-19.
Développé/Enveloppé Exercises (en avant)

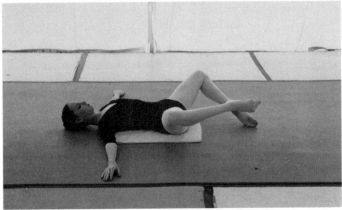

Exhibit 12-20.
Développé/Enveloppé Exercises (*à la seconde*)

Exhibit 12-21.
Attitude Devant Exercise (Starting position)

Exhibit 12-22.
Attitude Devant Exercise (Turned-out position)

Exhibit 12-23.
Leg Extensions (Starting position *à terre*)

Exhibit 12-24.
Leg Extensions (Starting position)

Exhibit 12-25.
Leg Extensions (*Arabesque* position)

Exhibit 12-26.
Leg Extensions (*Attitude derrière* position)

Exhibit 12-27.
V-Seat Position for Hamstrings (Starting position)

Exhibit 12-28.
V-Seat Position for Hamstrings (Turned to right)

Exhibit 12-29.
V-Seat Position for Hamstrings (Stretched to right)

Exhibit 12-30.
Partnered Hamstring Stretch

Exhibit 12-31.
Cabriole devant Exercise

Exhibit 12-32.
Modified Hurdler's Stretch

Exhibit 12-33.
Superficial Calf Stretch

Exhibit 12-34.
Deep Calf Stretch

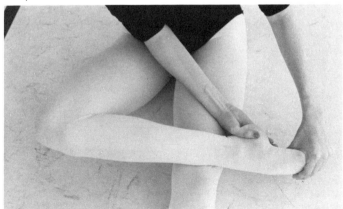

Exhibit 12-35.
Foot Stretch with Heel Block

Exhibit 12-36.
Standing *Demi-pointe* Foot Stretch

Exhibit 12-37.
Standing Deep Hip Flexor Stretch

Exhibit 12-38.
Standing Superficial Calf Stretch

Exhibit 12-39.
Standing Deep Calf Stretch

EPILOGUE
Another Look in the Mirror

For many young dancers, becoming a professional dancer is merely a dream—a vision of themselves in a mirror. Day in and day out they strive for perfection of the technique which opens the door to becoming an artist. Many dancers started at such a young age that dancing is virtually the *only* occupation they can envision.

The Mentorship of Dance

Sacrificing their youth to dance, boys and girls grow into adulthood without the diversifying experiences of a normal childhood and adolescence. Paradoxically, dancers are "old" for their age group while in adolescence, and disconcertingly naive as adults. At an early age, the classroom etiquette and structure force the child into becoming more disciplined than his or her non-dancing peers. Dance training is an undeniably maturing experience, even for those individuals who merely pass through a few years of lessons. Becoming a dancer requires talent along with the ability to take on serious adult responsibilities such as dependability, punctuality and committed decision-making.

At the age of eight, a girl may enter a pre-professional ballet school, and pursue a concentrated training program geared specifically for preparing her to become a professional dancer—usually in the resident company. During the next eight years, she will live for and dream of dance.

There will be little time or desire for anything else. This includes dating, studying, vacationing, making new friends outside of dance or just hanging out and having fun with friends. Dancing comes at the expense of formal education as well as a normal social or sexual development. These sacrifices may very well come back to haunt her after her retirement from dance.

If she is not weeded out during those early formative years, she will, at the ripe old age of 16 or 17, matriculate into the resident company, audition for another troupe or be cast into the streets to fend for herself.

For many years the school cares for and nurtures the personal and artistic growth of the young dancer, often acting like a surrogate parent to the child and adolescent. Sooner or later the parent-child mentorship begins to break down. The dancers resent being treated like children, and the teachers/directors fear the emergence of the assertive dancer who is his or her own decision-making person. The tradition in dance favors this bonding and mentorship as well as assures its dissolution. The same company school that nurtured the dancer into becoming an artist is often part of a company that abandons them when their bodies have broken under the yoke. When this grueling reality occurs, dancers often have a childlike, bewildered sense of betrayal.

This is not surprising, since a strong parent/child relationship exists in the classroom. In class teachers often refer to dancers as boys and girls—a derogatory categorization which frequently continues into the professional ranks. Professional dance is for men and women, not boys and girls.

Companies fear the growing assertiveness of professional dancers. When the dancers from the American Ballet Theatre went on strike a few years ago, they were made to feel like they were jeopardizing the financial future of the company as well as setting a dangerous precedent for dancers' rights. Some of the dancers were being paid less than the union stagehands, and I'm certain less than many administrators. The various rationalizations explaining this inequity always amazed me. These people would probably be *unemployed* if it were not for the talent and years of training and sacrifice of these underpaid dancers. No one in the audience buys a ticket to see administrators perform. Fortunately, the dancers stuck together and won, but I still don't think the company was happy with the transition of the complacent child/dancer into the assertive adult professional.

The Dancer's Rights

The dance profession needs to continue its efforts to assert the rights of dancers to fair employment practices, reasonable workloads and working conditions and equitable salaries. Audition and hiring standards should be clearly stated and followed, along with strict guidelines for promotion in rank and dismissal from the company. The amount of time spent in rehearsals and performance is now usually stipulated in the dancer's contract, and overtime work is compensated and controlled.

Abuses still abound in terms of excessive overtime and extensive rehearsal schedules during the season. Recently, a major East coast ballet company had 13 principal dancers out with injuries during a run of *A Midsummer Night's Dream;* most of the injuries were overuse injuries due to excessive overtime rehearsals along with a grueling performance schedule. In this situation, dancers need to put their foot down and work out more humane rehearsal/performance schedules with management.

The company school basically serves as a reservoir for preparing young dancers for the company by establishing a uniform technique, line and style. Senior students are groomed to become members of the company by learning and practicing much of the corps and soloist repertoire. This is a cheap way of making a dancer. While they are paying to train at the school, they are being rehearsed for the company. Seniors don't mind this at all—this is exactly what they wanted to do in the first place. But it constitutes an unfair practice to the professional members of the company, who are made to feel like they are replaceable. Much has been done to limit the misuse of school dancers by phasing them into the company through an apprenticeship program.

A professional dancer has very little job security. Basically, their position is solely dependent upon the opinion of the artistic director. Directors are looking for a particular type of dancer in terms of body type, style of dancing, technical facility and ability to integrate and interpret movement and music. Failure to meet any of these qualifications may result in dismissal. A few years ago, when Baryshnikov took over as director of ABT, a number of senior corps dancers were dismissed or their contracts were not renewed. As a result, some of these dancers filed grievances against the company on the basis of age discrimination. Age alone should not be grounds for dismissal. However, in all fairness to the director, it is in that person's power and prerogative to develop the company as he or she sees fit. If those are the rules, perhaps the rules should be changed.

> In one memorable scene from *Butch Cassidy and the Sundance Kid,* Butch Cassidy (Paul Newman) is about to have a knife fight with a huge, sadistic-looking ruffian. As the two approach one another, the bad guy pulls out a big bowie knife, which prompts the wide-eyed Butch to say, "Before we fight, we gotta make some rules."
>
> "Rules! There's no rules in a knife fight," screamed the villain, dropping his guard for a moment as he moved within striking distance.
>
> "You're right," replied Butch with a swift kick to the groin. Things are a lot fairer in fights when you have some rules.

The issue of salaries and benefits is a sore subject to dancers— almost as sore as their bodies. For an occupation that adds so much to the cultural well-being of a community, dancers are shamefully underpaid and overworked. One of the comments a corporation may use to entice a prospective upper management executive (they probably don't say it to assembly line workers) is, "Your family will love our city. You know we have a wonderful ballet company." Excuse me: a wonderful ballet company comprised of dancers living well below the poverty income level. We, of course, believe in supporting the arts in the community.

Many corporations in America do financially support dance companies. Efforts to enlist the help of the private sector of our economy in the war for wages have been moderately successful, but erratic and undependable. If corporations and businesses feel that dance companies make their community "more livable," they must help the dancers make a living. A $10,000 a year salary in New York City doesn't go too far; for that matter, it doesn't cut it in Detroit or Kansas City either. If you want art, you have to pay for it.

Other hot issues with dancers are healthcare and retirement benefits or the lack thereof. In most cases medical insurance for the dancer is minimal. Often, there is a physician in the community who works with the dance company, insurance underwriters and dancers to provide medical services at a reduced cost (I know many physicians who donate their services free to dancers). This isn't fair to the dancers or the doctors. Professional dancers should have full medical and dental insurance coverage provided by the company at little or no expense to the dancer. It shouldn't be on a "catch as catch can" basis.

Retirement benefits are a difficult point to resolve, because most dance careers don't last long enough to permit the accumulation of a retirement fund. Other than Nureyev or Fonteyn, when have you heard of a dancer lasting 25 years and retiring to Florida on an ample pension? It's hard to have a pension plan for a career that lasts ten years. Since dancers move from one company to another, a centralized retirement/retraining fund contributed to equally by the dancer and various companies would be highly beneficial. The fund could be supervised at no expense by either the dancer's union or a regulatory committee of dance representatives and financial advisors. The fund would be available either as a long-term retirement supplement or as a short-term educational fund for retraining or preparing the dancer for a new occupation. Sooner or later a dancer has to start all over either in another area of dance or in an entirely new field.

Sexism in Dance

Ballet beats out medicine for the perpetuation of blatant sexism and discrimination against women. Female dancers are the "worker bees" in the company, usually devoting much more of their lives into the dance without any possibility of moving into a management or director position of a major company after their careers. Paradoxically, the people who are most qualified for these jobs—in terms of experience, skills and talent—are the least likely to be considered.

Once upon a time in a large midwestern community, there was an old Russian ballerina who had dedicated her life to teaching, coaching and directing young dancers in the fine art of dancing. In many ways, Madame T. was what you would expect in a dance teacher: stern, authoritarian and demanding, with a distinctly noble bearing and thick Russian accent.

Madame T. was a most intriguing and accomplished woman, with an impressive dance pedigree. In

her youth she had danced in the Ballet Russe de Monte-
Carlo, and later came to the United States, like so many
other famous Russian dance emigrants, with her
brother, who was also a dancer and is now a teacher in
New York City. She became the city's tie to the illustri-
ous history of ballet, and the *grande dame* of classical
dance. For 20 years she worked hard to establish a civic
company of merit and worth—a source of community
pride and recognition. In 1978 she chose to retire and
turn the helm over to a new director.

The predominantly male board of directors selected
a middle-aged man of dubious talent and credentials to
take over the company. After a couple of years of awk-
ward, if not abominable, artistic transition and dwin-
dling community support, another director was found.
The new director declared the creation of a totally new
company, with no pre-existing ties to the former 20-year-
old company. Madame T.'s lifetime of dedication and
sacrifice were obliterated in one swift chauvinistic decision. Some of us have chosen not to forget.

Although the company has forgotten their roots, I
strongly believe that when it is to their advantage they
will remember. When they are 30 years old (if they make
it that far), someone in public relations will cleverly and
belatedly tack those 20 years back on and honor its
founder. You can raise a lot of money in a golden anni-
versary year. Unfortunately, Madame T. won't be there
to see this happy ending.

How many artistic directors of dance companies are female? In
regards to major ballet companies, the answer is simple. None.
Many companies were founded by women, but are now run by men.
For example, the Pennsylvania Ballet was founded and directed for
many years by Barbara Weisberg, but has been run by men since her
"retirement." Fortunately her enormous contribution to this company is still widely acknowledged and remembered. Granted there
are a number of female artistic directors of regional or civic companies. However, the big ballet companies are decidedly male domi-
nated in their boards, directorship and management. This is a most
curious development in an occupation which is predominantly female. Despite their years of experience, women are not being promoted to the top of the echelon. The situation looks and smells
suspiciously of discrimination.

The situation is quite different in modern dance companies.

Many famous dance companies were created and directed by women—Martha Graham and Twyla Tharp, to name only two. In fact there are numerous techniques, styles and pedagogies in modern dance developed exclusively by women; there are none in ballet. It is also generally true that the long-term career opportunities in modern dance—as a performer, university teacher, choreographer and director—are much better than in ballet. Although female artistic directors are needed and long overdue, I would advise only the toughest and most ambitious woman to take on the directorship of a major ballet company. Not only would it prove a most challenging task, but it would also make a fascinating biography.

Starting Over

Sooner or later, all dancers must start new careers. For some, their new career is a continuation of the old. They pursue jobs in dance-related fields such as teaching, choreography, production, management or administration. Teaching at a studio poses no particular problem for the retired dancer who has teaching skills and the ability, desire and patience to work with people. Many dancers don't have enough of these qualities to be successful; your reputation as an accomplished dancer will only go so far in the teaching trade before you are forced to comply with established standards of dance pedagogy. Teaching is a craft and talent that must be learned and nurtured just like dancing.

Going to a university and obtaining a degree in dance is mandatory for anyone considering teaching at a university, whether in ballet or modern. Dance departments are looking for dancers with professional performing experience *and* a master's degree in dance. These qualifications are hard to satisfy for ballet dancers who barely finish high school before entering a company. This requirement constitutes an expensive long-term re-education process for a ballet dancer. For modern dancers who have developed and trained in a university setting, the academic background is usually already there; it's the professional performing opportunities and experience that are harder to find.

Most dance departments are oriented predominantly towards modern dance due to the availability of qualified modern teachers, plus the fact that modern dance training is primarily university-based and ballet is company-based. Professorships in modern dance are therefore quite competitive, whereas positions for the ambitious ballet dancer with a master's degree are fewer in number but much less competitive.

Becoming a choreographer is a specialized talent in and of itself. For most dancers-turned-choreographers it is a hand-to-mouth existence. There is a significant demand for innovative choreography at a variety of levels ranging from classical dance to commercial productions. The training, encouragement and promotion of new choreographers is one of the strengths of the modern dance profession, and certainly one of the failures of the ballet profession. In either case, I think becoming a choreographer is the toughest post-dance occupation. Even good choreographers have found it difficult to establish themselves artistically and financially on a consistent basis. However, with the right connections, prolific talents and insensitivity to the comments of critics who have never danced a step in their lives, you may make it.

Costume, scenery and lighting design along with other production specialties demand specific talents, training and education. In some cities it may also require union membership. There are also training workshops and university degree programs in the fields of arts management and administration. On-the-job training is usually an essential part of these positions.

It is not the purpose of *The Dancer's Guide* to offer a complete listing of post-dance career opportunities and support organizations. The interested reader is referred to the lists in chapters 25 and 26 of Ellen Jacob's *Dancing: A Guide for the Dancer You Can Be* (Reading, Massachusetts: Addison-Wesley, 1981), and *The Guide to Career Opportunities in Dance* and *The Directory of Dance Colleges and Universities* published by the National Dance Association through the National Alliance for Health, Physical Education, Recreation and Dance (1900 Association Drive, Reston, VA 22070).

The Last Look in the Mirror

Throughout those years she believed in her desire and ability to dance. She wanted to be a dancer more than anything else, and, to that purpose, the teachers at her school or studio nurtured, coddled, pushed and prodded her into being the best dancer possible. When a dancer looks in the mirror, perhaps, he or she probably doesn't see the image of a Makarova, Farrell, Kirkland or Fonteyn (Baryshnikov, Martins or Bujones for men). Nevertheless, it is the image of a dancer with grace, line and movement. The flaws and faults are, of course, there for the dancer and perhaps a few others to see. But dance is not, nor does it claim to be, a perfect art. After all, it is a purely human manifestation. Dance personifies the noblest of human intentions—the *striving* for perfection in human expression and movement.

That vision of the dancer will always be indelibly printed in his or her mind. In fact, it will take a few years just to accept the body image of a normal person; a few pounds heavier, with a bit more of a curve here or there. But the dancer will adjust, adapt, acclimate and thrive. The same discipline, determination and concentration that serve so well in dance are the rudiments for success in other fields.

Those of us who have danced recall the excitement or pride at having put together those first basic steps into a simple dance. Like halted, stammering phrases in a beginning French class, we struggled with the mechanics of the new words in new phrases and worried later about their meaning, comprehension and fluency. As children of the dance, to be a dancer was to have arrived; as performers, to be an *artist* is the reality.

At the end of a long career, dancers must take that final look in the mirror and see the person, the artist, that they have become. They must reconcile their differences between early expectations and final product, come to terms with the internal image of the dancer and the external performer. Whatever the disparity, they leave dancing with the knowledge that they are the envy of many people who could only dream of dancing or view it from afar. Their accomplishment is unparalleled in terms of dedication, hard work, determination, sacrifice and sheer persistence. Dancing is fulfilling a dream—a vision of expressing oneself through movement and music. This is the primal purpose of becoming a dancer. What a wonderful benefit it is that as a dancer's career is fulfilled, our culture becomes more stimulating, meaningful and diverse, and our lives are enriched.

GLOSSARY OF MEDICAL TERMS

ABDUCTOR. A muscle which on contraction draws the bone to which it is attached away from the axial line of the extremity.

ADDUCTOR. A muscle that draws toward the midline of the body or a common center.

AMENORRHEA. Complete cessation of regular monthly menstrual flow. May be temporary or lasting.

ANOREXIA. A loss of appetite for food which appears as a symptom of mental illness (anorexia nervosa).

APOCRINE GLANDS. Sweat glands in the axilla and groin areas that lose some of their cellular structure while functioning. The interaction of bacteria on the skin with apocrine sweat produces the characteristic odor of perspiration.

APPENDICITIS. Inflammation of the worm-like process that comes off the cecum, the proximal end of the colon or large bowel.

ARTHROSCOPY. A technique for diagnosis or surgical manipulation within a joint by the insertion of a rigid metal tube containing a light and a small mirror, the arthroscope.

ASTHMA. A chronic condition characterized by spasms of the bronchial passages with wheezing, cough and shortness of breath. It can be aggravated by cold damp air, by infection in the respiratory system and by emotional disturbance. It is usually a form of allergic reaction. Exercise will aggravate it unless medication that will dilate the bronchial passages is taken.

206

ASTIGMATISM. Inability to focus sharply due to different refractions in several medians of the eyeball, usually due to change in the curvature of the cornea or the lens.

BONE SCAN. Use of radioactive material injected into a vein which provides concentration at injured bone site that can be identified on photographic plate.

BULIMIA. Morbid hunger associated with gross overeating, frequently followed by self-stimulated vomiting.

BURSA. A soft tissue sac lined with a synovial membrane which acts to reduce friction between tendon and bone, tendon and ligament or other structures.

CAT SCAN. An examination of the body in which serial section radiographs are made by a computer automated device. It enables you to see small details that may be easily obscured by the thickness of the part being scanned.

CERVICAL SPINE. Spine of the neck.

CHONDROMALACIA. Softness or degeneration of a cartilage, most commonly on the undersurface of the patella.

CONVULSIVE DISORDERS. Epilepsy is the major and common cause. Transient attacks of brain function with altered or complete loss of consciousness. In the grand mal form there is only loss of attention or a confused state. The cause is frequently unknown but the attacks may follow a brain injury. Good control can be obtained by regular use of prescribed medication.

CORONARY THROMBOSIS. A closing off of one of the arteries that supplies blood to the heart muscle. This may occur suddenly as the result of the formation of a blood clot in the artery or gradually as the result of the buildup of fatty degeneration in the wall of the artery.

CRUCIATE LIGAMENTS. Internal ligaments of the knee joint (anterior and posterior) that cross each other.

CYSTITIS. An infection in the urinary bladder.

DORSAL SPINE. Spine of the torso with attached ribs.

ECCRINE GLANDS. Sweat glands of the skin.

ECHOCARDIOGRAM. A recording on tape of the sound waves produced by the beating of the heart.

ELECTROCARDIOGRAM (EKG). A recording on tape of the electrical activity of the heart. The waves designated P., Q., R., S., T. and U. are related to the contractions of the auricles and ventricles of the heart.

EPIDEMIOLOGY. A sequence of reasoning concerned with defining the interrelationships between the variable causes and their effects in a particular environment.

EPIPHYSIS. A second bone-forming center of a long bone united by cartilage to main shaft in youth but by solid bone in late adolescence.

EXERCISE-INDUCED BRONCHOSPASM. Severe constriction of the bronchial passages stimulated by vigorous exercise in persons who may not have signs or symptoms of asthma at other times. Can be prevented or modified by taking appropriate medication before exercise.

EXTRA SYSTOLE. This is a premature contraction of the ventricle that may occur from excessive use of caffeine or cigarette smoking, but may also occur from damage to heart muscle.

FIBROSIS. Abnormal formation of fibrous connective tissue, as may happen around muscle as a result of chronic strain.

GENU RECURVATUM. Hyperextension at the knee joint.

GOITER, DIFFUSE TOXIC. Overactive thyroid, usually with only slight enlargement of the gland but with very rapid pulse and weight loss.

GOITER, EXOPHTHALMIC. Diffuse toxic goiter with protrusion of the eyeballs.

HALLUX. The great toe.

HEMORRHOIDS. A mass of dilated, tortuous veins beneath the skin in the region around the anus, both internally and externally.

HERNIA, FEMORAL. Protrusion of a peritoneal sac beneath the inguinal ligament and into the soft tissue of the upper inner thigh.

HERNIA, INGUINAL. Protrusion of a sac of peritoneum (lining of abdominal cavity) through the muscles and fascia of the abdominal wall in the region of the groin.

HYALINE CARTILAGE. The smooth and pearly cartilage that covers the articular surfaces of bones.

HYDROCOELE. Accumulation of serous fluid in a sac-like cavity formed by failure of closure of the peritoneum following the descent of the testis into the scrotum.

KERATIN. The tough protein in hair and nails that is insoluble in water.

KERATOLYTIC. Superficial skin removing.

LORDOSIS. An exaggeration of the natural forward curvature of the lumbar spine.

LUMBAR SPINE. Spine of the lower back attached to the sacrum of the pelvis.

MAGNETIC RESONANCE IMAGING. Shows serial sections of tissue based on the imaging of cells by means of directing a radio frequency pulse at portions of the body placed within a large magnetic field. Measures of the time required for the cell nucleus to return to a baseline energy state following this temporary stimulation can be translated by a complex computer algorithm to a visual image on a television monitor that can be reproduced graphically.

MATRIX. The basic substance from which hair and nails grow.

MELANOMA. A pigmented mole of the skin that has the potential of becoming malignant.

MENISCUS. An interarticular fibrocartilage of crescent shape found in joints, especially in the knee where there is a medial and lateral meniscus.

MESENTERIC ADENITIS. Inflammation of a lymph node in the fold of the peritoneum that connects the intestine to posterior aspect of the abdominal cavity. It is sometimes mistaken for the appendicitis.

MITRAL VALVE PROLAPSE. The leaflets of the mitral valve, that separate the left auricle of the heart from the ventricle in this condition, are slack, not tightly stretched. When the ventricle contracts to expel blood into the aorta the leaflets balloon back into the auricle, producing a click that can be heard with a stethoscope. This does not usually impair normal heart function or produce chest pain.

MONONUCLEOSIS. An infectious disease caused by a virus that involves the spleen and the lymph nodes in particular but can also affect the liver. Abnormal mononuclear cells are formed in the blood. It usually lasts from six to eight weeks and subsides with rest.

MYOPIA. Inability to see clearly at a distance of more than a few feet due to lengthening of the eyeball, which changes the point of focus of the lens.

NEPHRITIS. An infection of the kidneys.

OLIGOMENORRHEA. Diminution in normal menstrual flow which becomes scanty and intermittent.

OSTEOCHONDRAL FRACTURE. A fracture that involves bone and overlying cartilage, and is typically displaced.

PERIOSTEUM. The fibrous membrane that forms the covering of bone except on the articular surfaces where it is hyaline cartilage.

PLANTAR FASCIA. A fibrous membrane that covers the muscles on the sole of the foot.

REGIONAL ENTERITIS. Inflammation of the mesentery and the portion of intestine to which it is attached, which may be localized or extensive, involving large as well as small intestine. May be acute or chronic.

RHEUMATIC FEVER. An infectious disease that usually follows a streptococcal infection accompanied by high fever and painful swollen joints. It may affect the heart and cause chronic damage to the valves. More common in children.

SCOLIOSIS. A lateral curvature of the spine which may be caused by a lack of balance between muscles on both sides of the spine or by the body's attempt to keep the head level when the pelvis is tipped to one side because of a short leg. It may be corrected by the use of a brace temporarily and exercises and electric stimulation to strengthen the weak muscles.

Correction for a short leg requires the use of a heel lift in the shoe for that leg.

SESAMOID BONE. An ovoid bone in fibrocartilage in a tendon running over a bony surface. The patella is an example.

STRESS FRACTURE. A type of incomplete fracture resulting from repeated strain that does not involve the complete thickness of a bone. It causes pain and local tenderness at the fracture site. It may progress to a complete fracture if the strain is not reduced or prevented entirely. Slow to heal.

SUBLUXATION. An incomplete or partial dislocation of a joint. It frequently reduces itself spontaneously. If chronic, it may require surgical repair or fixation.

TACHYCARDIA. Runs of very rapid heart beats that may result from different causes. Needs medical investigation to establish control.

TROCHANTER. Either of two bony processes (greater and lesser) below the neck of the femur.

URETER. One of two mucous membrane lined passageways that carries urine from the kidney to the urinary bladder.

VARICOSE VEINS. Enlarged, twisted veins lying in the tissue beneath the skin, most commonly in the lower extremities.

GLOSSARY OF DANCE TERMS

ADAGE (Fr.), ADAGIO (Ital.). 1. A series or combination of dance exercises, usually performed in the center of the classroom to a slow musical tempo, comprising *pliés, tendus, dégagés, coupés, rond de jambes, développés, battements* and controlled pirouettes in all of the basic ballet positions and directions. The purpose is to display the grace, balance, line and skill of the dancer during slow, sustained movements. 2. In performance, that portion of the *pas de deux* in which the ballerina, supported, lifted or carried by her partner, performs delicately balanced *développés, pirouettes* and poses in *attitude* and *arabesque* along with a wide variety of lifts.

À LA SECONDE À LA HAUTEUR. See HAUTEUR.

ALLEGRO. A quick, lively musical tempo to which all springing and jumping movements, such as *jetés, sautés, entrechats,* and turns in the air are performed.

ARABESQUE. The dancer arches the body, balancing it over the supporting foot with the other leg extended posteriorly and the arms and hands extended forward to make the longest possible line from the tips of the fingers to the toes of the working leg. There are two to five basic variations, depending upon the particular style, involving different positions of the arms, the body and the relative extension of the supporting knee.

ASSEMBLÉ. A step of elevation in which the dancer brushes one foot into the air, pushes off the floor with the other, brings both legs together in the air and lands in fifth position.

ATTITUDE. The basic pose in which the dancer stands on one leg and brings the other leg up behind or forward at an angle of 90° from the midline, with the knee bent and the extremity externally rotated. The

212

arms are raised, and one may parallel the position of the raised leg in the same or the opposite direction.

BALLERINA. A principal female dancer in a ballet company. The first principal of a company may be called a prima ballerina.

BALLET. 1. A classic form of theatrical dance characterized by specialized movements, technique, traditions and vocabulary (See also CLASSICAL BALLET). 2. A theatrical spectacle that combines ballet dancing with specially composed music, costumes, scenery and lighting.

BALLET CLASS. The typical 90-minute classical ballet class is divided into an established sequence of exercises performed at the barre and in the center. Various combinations of *pliés, battements, tendus, battements dégagés, frappés, ronds de jambe, fondues, petits* and *grands battements* and *adagio* are incorporated into both phases of the class. Center work also involves an assortment of jumps, *batterie, pirouettes* and *tours* in *adagio, petit allegro* and *grand allegro* combinations.

BALLET MASTER OR MISTRESS. The person responsible for teaching classes, conducting rehearsals and reconstructing or creating the choreography of ballets in the repertoire.

BALLON. A desirable characteristic of elevation in which the dancer appears to ascend lightly, to sustain this position in the air, especially over some distance and to land very softly.

BARRE. The round horizontal bar, usually wooden, that is fixed to the wall of the classroom, studio, or rehearsal hall at a height of about three and one-half feet to provide hand support for the preliminary exercises of the class. These exercises have the general purpose of developing strength in the body, thighs, legs and feet and of freeing the limbs for a full range of rapid, easy motion. They may include *pliés, battements, développés, dégagés, fondues,* and *frappés* each of which has a special function. The bar is usually placed directly in front of a mirrored wall so that the dancer and ballet instructor may observe the movements clearly.

BATTEMENT. A beating movement of the working leg usually closing against the supporting leg. In a *grand battement,* the entire leg is raised from the hip into a position in the air (*en l'air*). A *petite battement* is a small beating by the foot against the ankle of the supporting leg. *Petits* and *grands battements* are performed at the barre and in the center. Many varieties may be performed at the bar: *arrondi* (circular), *dégagé* (outward up and down), *développé* (unfolding), *fondue* (sinking down), *frappé* (striking floor), *retiré* (foot withdrawn upward) and *tendu* (stretched working leg).

BATTERIE. A scissor-like movement of the legs during a jump. *Petite batterie* are small, sharply beaten movements of the legs as in *entrechats, brisés* and *jetés battus. Grande batterie* involve more exaggerated beats and greater elevation.

BRAS, PORT DE. *Bras* is the French word for arms. The four basic positions of the arms in the Vaganova (Russian) school, the six in the French school, and the nine in the Cecchetti method combine with the basic positions of the feet and placement of the head and shoulders (*épaulement*) to make up the stereotypical poses that are characteristic of ballet.

BRISÉ. Basically, a traveling *assemblé* with a beat. The dancer jumps from one or two feet, briskly beats the legs together while moving forward, backward, or sideways, and lands on one or two feet. Although there are a number of variations on the basic step, the most spectacular is the *brisé volé,* a combination of forward (*en avant*) and backward (*en arrière*) brisés that have a light "flying," or fluttering, appearance.

CABRIOLE. A beating movement of the fully extended legs in the air that starts and ends on the same foot. The dancer brushes the working leg either forward, backward, or sideways into the air, jumps off of the supporting foot, and strikes it against the top leg, propelling it higher, then lands on the original supporting foot.

CHAÎNÉS. A series of small half turns or *tours* on each foot performed in a straight line or while making a circle. May be done on *pointe* or *demi-pointe.*

CHANGEMENT DE PIEDS. The dancer springs up from the fifth position, changes the position of the feet in the air, and lands with the opposite foot in front.

CHASSÉ. A gliding or sliding step in which one foot appears to chase the other out of position. May be performed in any direction.

CHOREOGRAPHER. The person who designs and composes ballets or dances. Quite often the choreographer is also responsible for teaching ("setting") the sequence, style and intent of the movements or choreography to the dancers.

CLASSICAL BALLET. Historically, the classical ballet is characterized by such 19th century ballets as *The Nutcracker, Sleeping Beauty, Coppelia, Giselle* and *Swan Lake*. However, the term also refers to a 350-year-old tradition of a highly formalized and stylized ballet technique.

CORPS DE BALLET. The dancers who make up the bulk of the company or who appear only in groups in support of the principals on stage. Although their function was originally chiefly decorative and reactive, in recent times they have frequently been given individual and expressive roles. They now represent a school of performance from which some develop into featured dancers.

COUPÉ. A step in which one foot "cuts" the other away and takes its place.

CROISÉ. A standing position of the body in which the dancer forms an oblique angle or three-quarter view relative to the audience, and the extended leg appears crossed. *Croisé* is the opposite of *éffacé*, an open position of the legs seen from a three-quarter view.

DANSEUR, PREMIER. A principal male dancer in a ballet company.

DANSEUSE, PREMIÈRE. A principal female dancer in a ballet company.

DÉGAGÉ. The fully arched foot is pointed toward an open position in any direction.

DEMI-PLIÉ. The knees are bent as far as possible while keeping the heels on the floor.

DEMI-POINTE. The dancer rises onto the balls of the feet. Also referred to as three-quarter pointe.

DÉTIRÉ. The dancer holds the heel of the working leg in the air, extends the leg to the front (*en avant*) and carries it to the side (*à la seconde*).

DÉVELOPPÉ. A gradual unfolding of the leg as it is raised from the floor into full extension in the air.

ÉCARTÉ. The dancer presents a three-quarter or oblique view of the body to the audience with the working leg extended to the side.

ÉFFACÉ. The dancer faces one of the two front corners of the stage or studio and either extends the leg nearest the audience to the back or the farthest leg to the front.

ELEVATION. The ability of the dancer to raise the body from the floor and appear to sustain this movement.

ENCHAÎNEMENT. A combination of dance steps performed to a particular musical phrase.

EN DEDANS. A movement that originates in the back and circles to the front. In a pirouette, the turn is made toward the supporting foot.

EN DEHORS. A movement that originates in the front and circles toward the back. In a pirouette, the turn is made toward the working foot.

EN L'AIR. Any movement made in the air, as in *tour en l'air* or *rond de jambe en l'air*. Also, a raised position of the leg with the working foot elevated to the level of the hip (*à la hauteur*).

ENTRECHAT. A weaving or scissoring movement of the legs in the air. The dancer jumps into the air and rapidly crosses the legs in front and back. Each opening and closing of the legs is counted a beat. Performing 6 (*entrechat six*) and 8 (*entrechat huit*) beats in a single jump is fairly common; 10 (*entrechat dix*) is quite unusual.

ÉPAULÉ. The dancer presents a three-quarter view of the body with the arm and shoulder nearest the audience extended forward and the leg on the same side extended in *arabesque*.

FONDUE. The finish of a step or jump in which the dancer lowers the body by rolling down through the instep and bending the knee, ending in a *demi-plié* on one leg.

FOUETTÉ. A whipping motion in which the working leg moves the dancer around the supporting leg. These movements are usually performed *en l'air*.

FRAPPÉ. In the *battement frappé*, the dancer stands with the working foot wrapped around the ankle and forcefully extends that leg, allowing it to strike the floor during extension. It is the basic preparation exercise for developing a strong *jeté*.

GLISSADE. A gliding movement of the legs that often precedes a jump from a *demi-pliê*. It may proceed forward or backward.

GRAND BATTEMENT. See BATTEMENT.

GRAND BATTERIE. See BATTERIE.

GRAND PLIÉ. See PLIÉ.

HAUTEUR. The working leg raised at a 90° angle to the hip (*à la hauteur*). An angle of 135° to the front, side (*à la seconde*) or back is considered a good extension.

JETÉ. A jump from one foot to the other in which the dancer brushes the working leg into the air before landing upon it. It may be done in any direction and in a number of variations.

LINE. The aesthetic conformation or projected image created by the shape and proportion of the dancer's body as well as the positioning of the head, shoulders, arms, body and legs.

NOTATION. A system for recording dances in a series of symbols that can be interpreted to reproduce them without the presence of the choreographer who designed them. The system of Rudolf von Laban is most widely used.

PAS. The measured step of the dancer that may involve a simple or compound movement. A solo dance is a *pas seul* and a dance by two persons is a *pas de deux*.

PASSÉ (RETIRÉ). One leg is drawn up until the toes touch the back of the other knee. When the position is held as a pose, it is known as a *retiré*.

PETITE BATTEMENT. See BATTEMENT.

PETITE BATTERIE. See BATTERIE.

PIROUETTE. A complete turn of the body performed on one foot, either on *pointe* or *demi-pliê*. Usually, the working leg is bent so that the foot touches the side of the knee of the supporting leg, but it may also be in *seconde* position, attitude, or *arabesque*. Pirouettes may rotate either clockwise (outward, or *en dehors*) or counterclockwise (inward, or *en dedans*) relative to the supporting leg.

PLIÉ. The *plié* is a simple bending movement of the knees while bearing weight and maintaining external rotation of the lower extremity, as in a squat, and is the most fundamental movement in ballet. It is performed in all of the basic ballet positions and exercises. In the *grand plié*, the thighs are parallel to the floor at the lowest point of the *plié*. The heels remain on the floor only in the *seconde* position.

POINTE. The female dancer on *pointe* is dancing on the tips of her toes, principally the first and second digits. The aesthetic purpose is to create a straight line from the ends of the toes to the hip; an elongated, delicate image of the lower extremity.

PORT DE BRAS. See BRAS, PORT DE.

POSITIONS, BASIC BALLET. In the first position, the legs and thighs are turned outward at the hips so that the feet make an angle of 180° and the heels are touching. The second position is similar, but the heels are a shoulder width apart. In the third, the thighs and legs are the same but one foot is crossed in front of the other to make a right angle to it at the instep. The open fourth position is the same as the first, but with one foot forward of the other by a foot. The closed fourth position is taken from the third or fifth position, with one foot a foot in front of the other. In the fifth position, with the same turn-out the feet are parallel and close together, with the heel of the front foot at the joint of the great toe of the back foot.

RELEVÉ. Raising the body to a *pointe* or *demi-pointe* position. It may also be used to describe lowering of the heel of the working foot from *pointe* to the floor and raising it again to that position.

ROND DE JAMBE. A circling motion of the foot in which the dancer, moving the leg from the knee, inscribes a circle on the floor (*rond de jambe à terre*) or in the air (*rond de jambe en l'air*) with the pointed toe of the working foot. The movements are performed *en dedans* (counterclockwise) or *en dehors* (clockwise). A *grand rond de jambe en l'air* is a sweeping movement of the entire leg from the hip in a semicircle from front to back, or vice versa.

SAUTÉ. Basically, a hop using both legs or only one leg for propulsion. There is no jumping from one foot to the other as in the *jeté*.

TEMPS LEVÉ. Raising the body into the air by a spring from the feet.

TENDU (BATTEMENT TENDU). A pointing of the foot on the ground either to the front or to the side or to the back.

TOUR EN L'AIR. A movement in which the dancer jumps vertically in the air and turns one, two, or three revolutions. Usually, the *tour en l'air* starts and finishes in fifth position; however, it may also end in other poses such as *arabesque* or by dropping onto one knee.

TURN-OUT. External rotation of the lower extremities in dance. Perfect turn-out entails a total of 90° of external rotation in the hips, knees, leg, ankle and foot of each extremity so that when the heels are brought together they make a 180° angle. Although perfect turn-out is aesthetically desirable, it is not an anatomical or biomechanical commonplace.

For further reference to terms used in ballet, consult Technical Manual and Directory of Classical Ballet, *by Gail Grant (Dover: New York), 1982.*

INDEX

Art

Many great artists have died
without the appreciation of their peers
And many artists of transient fame
had their work expire with them.
Art does not necessarily transcend generations.
Its mortality, like its creators,
is capricious and varied.
What is certain is that it affects people's lives
enlightening, enriching, inspiring.
It is the vein of gold
in the coal of existence.

Robert Stephens